SOCIAL SCIENCE RESEARCH

A HANDBOOK

For Students

Gerald S. Ferman and Jack Levin

A SCHENKMAN PUBLICATION

HALSTED PRESS DIVISION

JOHN WILEY & SONS

New York — London — Sydney — Toronto

Copyright © 1975 by Schenkman Publishing Company
3 Mount Auburn Place, Cambridge, Mass. 02138

Distributed by Halsted Press Division, John Wiley & Sons, Inc.

Library of Congress Cataloging in Publication Data

Ferman, Gerald S.
  Social science research.

  Bibliography: p.
  1. Social science research—Handbooks, manuals, etc.
I. Levin, Jack, 1941- joint author. II. Title.
H62.F399   300′.1′8   74-22223
ISBN 0-470-25759-8

Printed in the U.S.A.

CONTENTS

PREFACE

We have written this book in order to introduce students to the concepts and conduct of quantitative social science research. Our general orientation is toward the *student* and his needs. But the particular usage of the book—whether as "cookbook" or as text—will depend in large part on the nature of the classroom situation to which the student is exposed and on the expectations of his instructor. For instance, the student who is enrolled in a course requiring his first-hand participation in the conduct of a research project might employ this book as a stage-by-stage guide for selecting a problem, conducting a theoretical analysis, collecting the data, performing statistical analyses, and writing a final report. Lacking a primary research experience, however, the student might turn to this work for a brief, textbook introduction to quantitative research methods in the social sciences.

Many individuals have made contributions to this work. We are indebted to Walter Olson and Morton Cowden, whose vigorous support of the experiment in social science learning was prerequisite to the completion of this project. We acknowledge the encouragement and support of Harvey Black, George Gitter, Herbert Greenwald, Norman Kaplan, William Levin, Bernard Phillips, A. Sheikh, D. Marshall, J. Bidinger, M. Bodine, M. Hough, T. Renahan, J. Radel, J. Darby, and J. Stein. We express our appreciation to Gregory Jost, whose assistance has been nothing less than essential. We are grateful for the dedication and efficiency of Joyce Shryack, Pat Coker, and Glenda Bliss, who carried out their secretarial duties with dedication and efficiency. Finally, we owe a profound debt of gratitude to our wives, Hanna Ferman and Flea Levin, for their influence, direct as well as indirect, has been consistently important to the outcome of our efforts.

Gerald S. Ferman
Western Illinois University
Jack Levin
Northeastern University

vii

CHAPTER 1: RESEARCH DESIGN—AN OVERVIEW

What is Research?

Before the student begins a discussion of research design, he would do well to acquire a basic understanding of the way that the social scientist goes about gathering information and answering questions about the nature of social and political reality. This process is known as *research*.

For many students, research may mean nothing more than looking up a lot of references in encyclopedias or going to an expert in the field for an opinion. To be sure, the social scientist doing research searches the literature in his field and often consults with his knowledgeable colleagues. Such procedures may yield new insights and generally increase the likelihood that the research will have relevance for the field.

But the primary method of social science research is based upon *systematically observing social or political reality*. This emphasis on careful and objective observation is what separates the approach of the social scientist from that of researchers in non-scientific fields such as religion or astrology,—researchers for whom the opinion of an authority or an argument that sounds reasonable may be evidence enough to establish the validity of an idea. Consider, for example, an astrology buff who consults his horoscope for advice; or a religionist whose spiritual answers are obtained by quoting passages from the Bible. By contrast, the social scientist is oriented to the empirical world; he establishes evidence by testing his ideas against experience, for example, by conducting a survey, a controlled experiment, or any of the other research methods to be discussed in this volume.

On the basis of the objectives of the social scientist, two kinds of research can be identified: (1) *fact-finding* and (2) *explanatory*.

Fact-finding research consists of a search for information with which a set of cases can be described. In general, the cases to be described are individuals located in a given social or political system. The student whose research venture is set up to collect facts focuses his attention on questions of "what"—for example: What are the attitudes of the people in my home town regarding aid to parochial schools? What do working class individuals think about the legalization of marijuana? What can be said about the patterns of neighborliness in a large urban community?

In contrast to its fact-finding counterpart, explanatory research aims at discovering "why." As a result, it focuses centrally upon explaining social or political phenomena with answers of a theoretical nature: Why do certain persons tend to support traditional values? (As a tentative answer, we might study the *relationship* between affluence and commitment to hard work and individualism). Why are some individuals extremely prejudiced against minorities? (As a tentative answer, we might study the *relationship* between authoritarian child-rearing practices and attitudes toward blacks). Or, why are some children more aggressive than others (As a tentative answer, we might study the *relationship* between television-viewing and aggressive play).

In a sense, both fact-finding and explanatory research can be regarded as descriptive; since both focus on sense-perceived behavior, usually touch, sight, or hearing. However, fact-finding research operates at a lower-level of description, insofar as it seeks merely to isolate valid information and provide a narrative of what exists. This is an important goal, but is usually regarded as the first step with respect to research objectives. By contrast, explanatory research operates at a fuller or higher level of description which includes making relational statements containing *reasons* or *causes* for behavior. In other words, the fuller a description, the more likely it is to include explanation (Van Dyke, 1960).

Both fact-finding and explanatory forms of research can generate useful and important information about social and political phenomena. Involvement with either may serve as a worthwhile learning experience for the student of social science. It should also be noted, however, that worthwhile explanatory research generally requires greater creativity, imagination, and skill and delivers a bigger payoff for social science than does a purely fact-finding research effort. Finding out "what is" tends to have neither the excitement nor the challenge of finding out "why."

Research Design—What Is It?

The research design can be thought of as a *preliminary* and *flexible* strategy of investigation or plan of action. For many of the research projects in social science, the research design will include: (1) a statement of the problem to be investigated, (2) a theoretical analysis of the problem, and (3) plans for testing the hypothesis. A detailed discussion of these components of research design can be found in subsequent chapters of this book.

As we shall see, the research design is a useful device for the student of social science who sets out to conduct a research project; for it requires him to convert his vague ideas and problems into the precise terms of a researchable project. In order to do so, the student must combine the ingredients of creativity and discipline to produce a sensible (and manageable) strategy for research. Moreover, the research design provides the direction for carrying out specific research tasks. Having constructed a research design, the student has a concrete notion of what data he wishes to collect, how he plans to process and analyze the data, and what findings he needs for the purpose of accepting or rejecting his hypothesis. In sum, with the aid of a research design, the student saves valuable time and energy by avoiding unnecessary or redundant research activities.

It should be emphasized here that the research design is a tentative, flexible plan for research that may be altered as the research actually proceeds and unforeseen problems or insights come to light. But the importance of the research design cannot easily be exaggerated, since it provides a means whereby the student's research objectives can be efficiently pursued. No wonder that a colleague remarked recently that a social scientist who has three dollars for research would be wise to spend two dollars on his research design!

What's Ahead

The student has been given an overview of social science research and a preview of the major components and objectives of research design. In subsequent chapters, this general picture will be translated into some practical guidelines for the conduct of social science research. The first task is to select a problem to research.

CHAPTER 2: SELECTING A PROBLEM

How do we go about locating a researchable problem? The most direct way is to ask questions. In the context of explanatory research, for example, we might ask: *Why* do certain kinds of people vote for a particular political party? *Why* do nations make war on one another? *Why* are crimes committed?

Each of the foregoing questions designates a broad *problem-area*—voting behavior, violence and war, or criminality—in which a student may be interested. But none of these questions is precise enough yet to be regarded as capable of being researched. Such general questions must be further clarified and focused in order to *delineate the problem-area and suggest pertinent research activities*. To illustrate: an interest in voting behavior might be focused by asking, What is the effect of affluence on voting behavior? An interest in war and violence might be focused by asking, What is the influence of the socio-economic conditions of a nation on its willingness to go to war? Or, an interest in criminality might be focused by asking, What is the influence of family structure on criminality?

The importance of precisely stating the research question is nicely illustrated in the context of the following fact-finding research project:

It is an old and wise saying that 'a problem well put is half-solved' . . . we have to put a great deal of thought into the formulation of our questions if we hope to get anything out of an effort to answer them. For example; suppose that in the course of an ordinary conversation you ask a friend, 'How many people live in your house?' . . . Would you be willing to ask the same question . . . [if] you are conducting an important housing survey? . . . Chances are that you would not. A moment's consideration shows that you would be concerned with such questions as these: Should a son who is away at college . . . be included . . . ? Should a boarder who travels during the week . . . be included? Or the maid who sleeps in

three nights? ... It becomes clear that the more carefully the problem is formu-
lated, the more assurance we gain in obtaining a satisfactory solution (Ackoff,
1953, p. 14).

Selecting a Problem

Despite the large number of unresolved general issues in social science,
it is not always an easy task to choose a specific problem that is clearly in
need of research. For this purpose, therefore, the student might find it
useful to consider the following sources: (1) Personal experience, (2)
examination of the literature, and (3) discussion with friends and experts.

(1) Personal Experience

A simple but useful method of generating researchable problems is to
take the "armchair approach" of *thinking* about personal experiences and
observations. The student may recall, for example, having discussed with
friends or relatives the merits of controversial topics such as socialized
medicine or premarital sex. The very act of thinking about such experiences
often helps to generate interesting questions. Why are certain individuals so
extreme in their objections to socialized medicine or permarital sex? Might
family or educational background have something to do with such attitudes? Regarding socialized medicine, it might be proposed that families
having high socio-economic status tend to react in a hostile manner to
government enterference in a free enterprise system. Concerning sex before
marriage it might be argued that parochial school attendance tends to be
associated with negative feelings about having premarital sexual experiences.

(2) Examination of the Literature

Researchable ideas can often be culled from the table of contents of
textbooks, journal articles, and from class notes. A recent issue of the
journal *Social Problems* contains the article, "Father Absence and Self
Conception Among Lower Class White and Negro Boys (Hartnagel,
1970)." From the title of this article alone, we can begin to explore some
related questions: Does the father-absent family structure have an adverse
impact on the child's self conception? Is it more negative under such
circumstances? Or, does the father-absent family have a different effect on
lower-class white than on lower-class black children? Upon actually reading

this article, we might be led to wonder whether different results might have been obtained among *middle-class* children who were socialized in the context of a father-absent family. We might expect (or hypothesize), for example, that the self conception of the middle-class child is not so much influenced by family structure, since he can find reinforcements in ways that are less available to his lower-class counterpart.

Consider another example: In reviewing the title (and subheadings) of Chapter 6 of *Public Choice in America.* "How Policy is Made: Bargaining Among Politicians," (Mitchell, 1971) one might wonder why a certain group of Americans (for example, farmers) benefit from public policy more than another group of Americans (for example, ghetto inhabitants). After reading the part of this chapter concerning bargaining resources, the student may come up with the hunch that the greater the bargaining resources of a group (for example, their social status, effect on election outcomes, cohesiveness, etc) the greater the benefit from public policy it tends to receive.

There are numerous social science journals to which a student can go in order to explore a particular problem for research. The most accessible of such journals in sociology and political science include:

SOCIOLOGY	POLITICAL SCIENCE
American Sociological Review	American Political Science Review
American Journal of Sociology	Midwest Journal of Political Science
Social Forces	Journal of Politics
Social Problems	Political Science Quarterly
Sociology and Social Research	Review of Politics
Sociological Quarterly	Western Political Quarterly
Social Science Quarterly	World Politics
Society	Public Opinion Quarterly

(3) Discussion with Friends and Experts

The student who discusses his research project with friends or experts may come to better understand his areas of interest and to express those interests in terms of researchable problems as opposed to vague abstractions or general ideas. In an exchange of ideas with his fellow students or with teachers, for example, a student who is interested in revolutions in developing nations may begin to think in terms of their causes, and, in so doing, may generate the hypothesis that revolutions are more likely to occur under economic instability (that is, the more unstable an economy, the greater the probability of a revolution—coup d'etat). In a similar way, the student who is interested in understanding the "generation gap" might ask his classmates and friends a series of questions having to do with how well they get along with their parents. This inquiry might lead him to speculate that students who agree with their parents regarding important values (such as about sex, work, and politics) tend to get along better with them than do students who disagree with their parents regarding important values.

Criteria For Selecting a Problem

In order to select a problem for research, the student must be able to recognize the "right" problem when it comes along. The criteria to apply in selecting a problem usually include: (1) personal interest, (2) significance, and (3) managability.

(1) Personal Interest

In choosing among problems for his research project, the student should ask: "Does this problem interest me? Am I really interested in searching for an answer?" If the response on either count is "no," then the student would be wise to look for another problem.

There is no reason why research should not be fun. But it cannot be regarded as such by a student who has little or no interest in his topic. Moreover, as a practical matter, the student who lacks the motivation to conduct research tends to do an adequate job at best—a job that reflects little about his capabilities and sheds little additional light on the issue which his research has raised.

(2) Significance

Closely related to the criterion of personal interest is the question of whether or not the problem is a "significant" one. From a purely personal standpoint, of course, a student's interest in the problem is by itself sufficient justification for conducting the research.

Intellectual curiosity works in different ways for different people: a certain student may seek to test some theoretical notion that he has, for example, the relationship between age and political conservatism or the relationship between relative deprivation and prejudice against minority groups. Another student may wish to experiment with the research method itself (for example, survey research) in order to learn more about it or simply to master its techniques.

It is also desirable for the research venture to be of interest to people other than the student who conducts the research project. Significance is often defined in such terms. For example, research which seeks to uncover campus attitudes regarding twenty-four hour access of both sexes to all dormitories might yield useful information for those who are attempting to revise dormitory regulations in the direction of greater liberalism. In the same way, a study of the problems experienced by the tenants of a particular public housing project might turn out to have important implications for those who seek to upgrade the quality of life among the poor. The point we are trying to make is only that research can be *important* as well as interesting—that the results generated from a student's research project can be of value not only in the context of the course for which it was conducted, but for the wider community as well.

A final point to consider with respect to significance is whether the student's research is capable of serving as a vehicle whereby his understanding of social or political structure and process might be enhanced. This is the primary educational objective of research; it can be carried out to the extent that the student finds *links* between his own research and the existing literature in his field. For example, a student might investigate the complaints of public housing tenants about the public housing authority or the project manager as a way of studying the larger issue of the treatment of stigmatized clients by a service bureaucracy. In this way, his study immediately becomes related to many other studies of the same issue, whether they are concerned with the treatment of the blind by a government agency, blacks by a child guidance clinic, or lower status patients by a hospital. Likewise, a student might focus upon attitudes regarding access of both sexes to dormitories in an effort to discover factors associated with the acceptance or rejection of more equalitarian sex roles. In this case, the student relates his own project to a large body of literature concerned with conceptions of sex roles.

The same point can be illustrated from the perspective of political science:

> The sophisticated political science major may well be able to fit his own research paper into current theorizing about politics. But, if they stop to think about it, students with no background whatsoever in political science will still be able to see broader political implications in the topics they have chosen. Thus the

role of the National Association of Manufacturers in the enactment of a particular piece of foreign aid legislation is by itself interesting enough. It assumes even greater significance, however, to the extent that it can be reviewed as a case study of domestic constraints on foreign policy, or of interest group behavior or even of the internal organizational tasks faced by voluntary groups seeking to attain goals in an environment (Merritt and Pyszka, 1969).

(3) Problem Managability

Personal interest and significance are important criteria for the selection of a researchable problem. But the student should also beware of taking on *too much work* by tackling a problem that demands more time and energy than he has to give to it.

Fulfilling the most modest research objectives generally requires careful planning and time-consuming efforts to collect, code, and analyse a body of data. In this connection, a commonplace "roadblock" to the completion of a research project has to do with securing the data. Specifically, the student will all too often fail beforehand to verify the availability of the data he needs in order to carry out the research and test his expectations. For example, a student who wishes to study the "underground" press may discover too late that a representative sample of underground periodicals cannot be obtained within a reasonable period of time (during a one-semester course). A student who needs to interview a sample of black ghetto respondents may find that many black Americans are suspicious of his intentions and consequently refuse to cooperate with him. Such problems should be anticipated and overcome in the research design stage, that is to say, before the project is actually carried out.

What's Ahead

To this point, we have considered the early stages in the research process wherein (1) general questions are asked in order to identify a problem-area and (2) more precise questions are derived, so that attention can be focused upon a part of the problem-area of interest to the student researcher. If the process has been successful, it should lead him to a researchable problem: one that is precisely stated, significant, managable, and interesting from a personal standpoint. It is the primary purpose of the next chapter to examine that phase in the sequence of research activities known as the theoretical analysis, a phase in which the researcher comes up with a tentative answer for his research problem.

Exercises

1) Following the suggestions given in Chapter 2, identify three research problems taken from any problem-areas in social science.

2) Evaluate the problems derived in Exercise #1 above in terms of the criteria of personal interest, significance, and managability. On this basis, to what extent can the problems you have selected be regarded as effective from a research standpoint?

CHAPTER 3: THEORETICAL ANALYSIS

Before setting out to collect his data and obtain results, the student must place his research problem into an appropriate theoretical context. In so doing, he seeks to derive a meaningful way to explain or understand the problem he studies, making sure at the same time that his research project can be linked to the existing social science literature.

As a result of the functions it performs, the theoretical analysis can be regarded as an important stage in the process of doing research. It cannot be conducted, however, without having some understanding of *concepts*, *variables*, and *propositions*, the basic elements that go to make up a theoretical structure. We begin our discussion by focusing on the nature of concepts.

What Is A Concept?

A "concept" is an abstraction from reality, a term that designates a class of phenomena or certain characteristics shared by a class of phenomena (Social Science Research Council, 1954). Social science concepts include alienation, government, neighborliness, activism, conservatism, capitalism, authoritarianism, prejudice, socialization, and role, to mention just a few.

As abstract ideas, concepts assign a name to any general element in the experience of an individual (Van Dyke, 1960). For instance, the name "cow" is given to a structural form having a certain type of head and body. In the same way, the name "government" designates a certain set of political structures and processes. It has already been noted, however, that only some concepts refer directly to a class of phenomena: things that have a specified form such as cow or government. Other concepts specify certain characteristics that are shared by a given class of phenomena. To illustrate, the concepts "height" and "weight" can be used to characterize the class of phenomena known as cows, while the concept "totalitarianism" is characteristic of a class of phenomena referred to as governments (Social Science Research Council, 1954).

Real and Nominal Definitions of Concepts

The definition of a concept may be regarded as real or nominal. If *real*, a name or symbol is assigned to the *nature* of a phenomenon. If, however, the definition is *nominal*, then a name or symbol is assigned to certain features of interest to the researcher, rather than to the intrinsic nature of a phenomenon. To illustrate this distinction, consider the concept "cow" which has been assigned to indicate a certain form, the nature of a particular animal. We can change the label or symbol "cow" if we wish, but the nature of the form remains unchanged (that is, it still has a head, four legs, tail, etc.). In contrast, a nominal definition reflects arbitrariness not only with respect to the symbol or label, but also with respect to the characteristics we are willing to assign to it. Democracy may be defined as a political system with a president possessing certain powers, as a system with competitive political parties, as a system guaranteeing rights to minorities, as a system in which the majority has the final say on policy, or in scores of other somewhat overlapping ways. Thus, we can change the label (for example, from "Democracy" to "pluralism," "freedom," or "blobv") *as well as* the particular characteristics we associate with it. For this reason, the definition of "democracy" can be regarded as nominal.

It is far too common for students to believe that all social science concepts are real concepts. Yet this is generally not at all the case. Especially in regard to theoretical concepts, the labels or symbols used by the social scientist designate a part of reality that interests him. That is to say, a label or symbol means what the researcher wants it to mean because he finds it *useful*, in a research context, to reflect a particular set of characteristics of reality. Thus, concepts such as authoritarianism, justice, or socio-economic status mean what the researcher defines them to be, the definition being evaluated in terms of its usefulness. The proper question becomes: does grouping particular characteristics together under a given label facilitate an understanding of the subject matter? In a social research context, "affluence" may be defined according to the amount of money that a respondent earns per annum. In the context of psychological research, however, a researcher may define "affluence" in terms of perceived or expected wealth (for instance, "How much money do you expect to be earning per annum?"). Both uses of the concept "affluence" are legitimate if they serve the needs of the particular investigation.

Conceptual and Operational Definitions

To this point, we have considered only the conceptual definition of a term—that definition which designates its abstract or general meaning. In order to be useful in the context of social science research, however, many terms must also be operationally defined. The *operational definition* specifies the specific research procedures by which a conceptual definition can be applied over objects, things, or persons. For example: "democracy" can be defined as the degree to which citizens determine policy. This cannot be measured directly, however. That is to say, we cannot by this definition measure the "degree of democracy" characterizing a number of political systems; it is simply too broad and vague to be applied to the specific instances that occur in research. Operationally, however, "democracy" can be measured by selecting and applying certain *indicators* of the degree to which citizens determine policy: for example, (1) citizen attitudes about whether citizens determine policy in their country, (2) the level of participation in political activities, (3) a measure of the "fit" between public opinion and public policy on several issues. Similarly, authoritarian child-rearing can be conceptually defined with reference to harsh and threatening punishment of the child by his parent. Operationally, authoritarian child-rearing practices might be indicated by (1) the amount of spanking and yelling as reported by the parent or the child, or (2) the total amount of punishment as reported by the parent or the child.

As we have seen, then, the researcher—by his choice of an operational definition—can determine the degree or level of a concept across many units (for example, across nation-states or parent-child relationships). But how does the researcher know whether his operational definition of a term actually corresponds to its conceptual definition? To what extent does the operational definition actually "get at" the concept that he seeks to measure?

Such questions focus upon the *validity* of an operational definition, an important issue which has been known to generate intense controversy. Consider, for example, the highly publicized debate regarding the "fit" between conceptual definitions of intelligence and its operational definition in the IQ test. What many individuals fail to realize is that validity is a matter of degree: few if any of the operational definitions in social science can be regarded as perfectly valid.

Though there is no hard and fast rule to apply here, the researcher should attempt to verify the degree of "fit" between his conceptual and operational definition. There are times when he can rely for this purpose upon *face validity* whereby the operational definition *looks* "on the face of it" as though it measures the concept under study. Thus, an operational definition of "affluence" whose conceptual definition involves the degree of wealth possessed by any given individual might *reasonably* include the total income of an individual as specified on his Federal Income Tax form. Tremendous face validity! Yet, even this apparent "fit" leaves something to be desired, since some personal wealth never gets reported in Federal Tax forms. It is unfortunately true that face validity is not always sufficient.

In addition to face validity, there are several useful procedures for checking the validity of an operational definition. Those most likely to be employed in student research are (1) consulting experts, (2) making comparisons with a valid measure, and (3) using a known group.

Let us illustrate the foregoing strategies by considering how to establish the validity of an operational definition of academic achievement as indicated by scores on a particular achievement test:

(1) Consulting experts. We might compare the test scores of a group of students with the evaluations of their teachers. To the extent that the test is a valid indicator of achievement, high scorers should be highly evaluated by their teachers, whereas low scorers should be evaluated poorly.

(2) Making comparisons with a valid measure. We might compare the test scores of a group of students with their scores on another achievement test, the validity of which has already been established. To the extent that our test is valid, high scorers on one test should be high scorers on the other; low scorers on one test should be low scorers on the other.

(3) Using a Known group. We might administer our achievement test to known groups of "superior" and "inferior" students. To the extent that our test is a valid indicator of achievement, the superior students should receive high scores, whereas the inferior students should get low scores.

How to Increase the Value of a Concept

Assuming that clarity can be maintained, the usefulness of a concept is often increased by moving it to a higher level of abstraction, so as to include a larger number of phenomena. The concept "cow" is at a low level of abstraction as compared with the more abstract concept "animal" which logically implies a whole series of lower level concepts such as "cow," "sheep," and "pig." In the same way, the abstract concept "aggression" might include such diverse activities as war, suicide, riots, protest, boxing, prejudice, and verbal debate. If we explain something about the nature of aggression, then we explain something about each of the lower level concepts (for example, war, suicide, riots, protest, prejudice, boxing, and verbal debate) as well. If, however, we explain something about the nature of a lower level concept such as "prejudice," it may or may not also apply to other lower level concepts such as boxing and war or to aggression generally. By working with more abstract concepts, we increase the scope of our explanations: a worthwhile strategy for the social scientist who seeks to understand as much as he can about the nature of human behavior.

What is a Variable?

We have seen that a concept is an abstraction from reality. A *variable* is a concept; but a concept which in a given research project takes on two or more values or degrees. That is to say, it is a concept that *varies*. In social science research, variables include alienation (high/medium/low), government (democratic/totalitarian). neighborliness (high/low), political orientation (radical/liberal/moderate/conservative/reactionary), prejudice (prejudiced/ tolerant), and intelligence (a range of IQ scores), to mention only a few.

Not all concepts can be regarded as variables. When a concept lacks the capacity to vary; that is, when—in a given research project—it can have only one value, it is known as a *constant*. To illustrate: the researcher who studies the effect of education on political participation may choose to *hold constant* income, in an effort to *control for* its influence on the relationship between education and participation. To achieve this effect, he may examine only those respondents earning roughly the same amount of money annually, but who vary with respect to educational achievement and level of political participation. In this way, he treats income as a constant and education and political participation as variables.

Given the nature of the foregoing illustration, the student may already see that "one researcher's variable is another researcher's constant." For the researcher who seeks to study the effect of income on political participation, it may be appropriate to hold constant education. In this case, education is treated as a constant, while income and political participation are treated as variables.

Kinds of Variables

We can identify several kinds of social science variables according to whether they possess (1) nominal, (2) ordinal, or (3) interval properties.

(1) Nominal Variables

Nominal variables indicate sameness or differentness with respect to a given characteristic. They group individual cases together into separate categories but do not signify grading, scaling, or ranking for such qualities as better or worse, higher or lower, more or less. Many nominal variables are dichotomous, since they take two values or categories as numerically represented by (1) and (2) or by any two numbers that may be assigned. Examples of dichotomous nominal variables include: Sex: (1) Male and (2) Female; Marital Status: (1) Married and (2) Unmarried; Government: (1) Totalitarian and (2) Non-Totalitarian; Delinquency: (1) Delinquent and (2) Non-Delinquent. Other nominal variables include Religion: (1) Protestant, (2) Catholic, and (3) Jewish; Political Orientation: (1) Radical, (2) Liberal, (3) Moderate, (4) Conservative, and (5) Reactionary.

(2) Ordinal Variables

At the next level of complexity are variables which *order* a researcher's cases in terms of the degree they possess any given characteristic. For *ordinal variables*, the order in which numbers are assigned to categories has significance for depicting the degree to which a characteristic is present. As an example, consider the measurement of rank in a graduating class of 10 students:

Student	Rank In Class
Joe	1
Mary	2
Ruth	3
Al	4
Stan	5
Fred	6
Charles	7
Bonnie	8
Robert	9
Heidi	10

As shown above, Joe finished "first," Mary finished in second place, whereas Heidi was in the tenth position. It would obviously destroy the ordinal property of this variable to arbitrarily rearrange the numbers (for example, giving Charles a "2" despite his seventh place finish).

(3) Interval Variables

Though ordinal variables yield information about the order of categories, they do not indicate the *degree of difference* between them. By contrast, *interval variables* signify the order of categories, while indicating the exact distance separating them. Interval variables can take on an *infinite number of values*, permitting individual cases to be assigned *scores*. For example, family income might be noted as being exactly $12,967.79, or a student's performance on the College Board Exam might be indicated as a score of 562. If another student obtains a score of 750 on the same exam, then we can determine not only that this second score is better than the first, but exactly *how much* better ($750 - 562 = 188$ points better).

The characteristics of interval variables in contrast to ordinal variables can be illustrated by applying both procedures to the same phenomenon—student test scores.

Ordinal Variable:

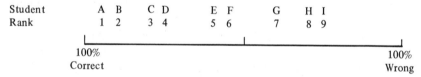

Rank-Ordering of Nine Students on a Test
(100 Single Point Questions)

Student	A	B	C	D	E	F	G	H	I
Rank	1	2	3	4	5	6	7	8	9

100%
Correct

100%
Wrong

One can conclude that the first score (a) is greater than the second (b), the second greater than the third (c), etc. *How much greater*, however, is not known from this type of variable scaling.

Interval Variable:

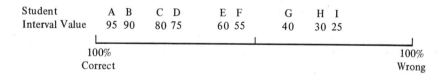

Test Scores of the same nine students

Student	A	B	C	D	E	F	G	H	I
Interval Value	95	90	80	75	60	55	40	30	25

100%
Correct

100%
Wrong

One can say that the first score (a) is greater than the second (b), etc. plus *how much greater—5 percentage points/or, in this case, 5 more questions correct.*

Choosing a Variable Strategy

Some variables can be assigned numbers in only one way. For instance, the nominal variable "sex" has two possible categories, male and female. Other variables can be assigned numbers in several different ways. Many can be treated as variables having two, several, or an infinite number of values. To illustrate: we could ask a respondent to give his annual income with only two categories (1 = $10, 000 or less; 2 = $10, 001 or more), with several categories (1 = $2000 or less; 2 = $2001 − $5000; 3 = $5001 − $7000; 4 = $7001 − $10, 000; 5 = $10001 − $15000; 6 = $15001 or more), or by asking for the exact amount of his annual income.

Assuming that a researcher has the choice to make, how should he go about determining the form that his variable will take? How many categories should he employ? The strategy of the student depends upon the nature of his research objectives. If he wishes to pinpoint precise differences between individual cases, then interval variables would be most likely to yield the desired result. If, however, only rough approximation will do, then the student might consider treating the research variable as dichotomous or in terms of a limited number of categories. Nominal and ordinal variables are generally easier to construct than are their interval-level counterparts.

Consider the following situation. A student wants to determine whether or not his friends support the President. If this is the extent of specificity desired, the student might ask his friends to respond to the President in terms of two categories: 1=in favor and 2=opposed. If, however, the research objective calls for greater precision, the following five-point-scale might be more appropriate:

  1=Strongly In Favor
  2=In Favor
  3=Neither In Favor nor Opposed
  4=Opposed
  5=Strongly Opposed

We shall return to questions related to variable strategy in Chapter 4.

What is a Proposition?

Variables can be combined in order to produce *propositions*—statements of relationship between two or more variables. As an illustration, consider that the variables "frustration" and "aggression" can be related to form the proposition: "The greater the level of frustration, the greater the aggression." Likewise, the variables "family structure" and "delinquency" can be combined in the proposition: "Children from one-parent-families are more likely than children from two-parent-familes to engage in delinquent behavior."

Many propositions are causal statements, in that they seek to explain the occurrence of a given phenomenon. Such propositions usually contain a variable to be explained or accounted for known as the *dependent variable* as well as a presumed cause referred to as the *independent variable*. In the proposition, "The greater the level of frustration, the greater the aggression," "frustration" serves as the causal or independent variable, whereas "aggression" is treated as the effect or dependent variable. Similarly, in the proposition, "Children from one-parent-families are more likely to engage in delinquent behavior than are children from two-parent families," "family structure" is regarded as the independent variable, while "delinquency" is the dependent variable.

Not all conceptions of cause and effect are appropriate for social science research. In particular, the student researcher should avoid conceiving of causal statements in which the presence of an independent variable is treated as being *sufficient* for the subsequent occurrence of a dependent variable. Such *absolute* statements of cause and effect ignore the fact that the relationship between any given independent and dependent variable always depends on its environment (Ackoff, 1953). For instance, the relationship between education and income depends upon the existence of a certain economic environment—an environment in which extra monetary reward for advanced training is permitted. Therefore, this proposition would not hold under pure communism, wherein each citizen is rewarded according to his particular needs.

It should be noted, moreover, that not all statements of relationship between variables are of the cause-effect variety. Such non-causal propositions take the form of *correlations*, in which their variables are associated, though not in a causal manner.

To illustrate:

. . . in one large city it was discovered that people who live in neighborhoods in which there is a heavy soot-fall are more likely to get tuberculosis than people who live in neighborhoods with less soot-fall . . . On the basis of the correlation between soot-fall and tuberculosis one researcher concluded that soot-fall was a producer of tuberculosis. Subsequent research revealed that this was not the case; it showed that dietary deficiencies are among the producers of tuberculosis. Further, it revealed that (these) deficiencies are likely to occur most frequently among low income groups . . . (and these) groups are likely to live in low-rent districts. Districts become low-rent, among other things because of heavy soot-fall (Ackoff, 1953, p. 68).

Thus, as a result of an *indirect linkage* between soot-fall and tuberculosis, these variables were related though not causally, and were directly associated with the presence of dietary dificiencies characteristic of low income life styles.

Establishing Cause and Effect

The main lesson to be learned from the foregoing example is that "correlation does not always indicate causation." If prejudice against minorities tends to decrease as formal education increases, we cannot be sure that one variable causes the other, despite their association. On the other hand, "causation *always* requires correlation." That is to say, two variables that are causally connected can be expected to vary together. If formal education actually tends to reduce prejudice against minorities, then we can expect that prejudice will decrease as formal education increases.

Despite its importance, then, correlation alone is not enough to establish the presence of a causal proposition, one that contains an independent and a dependent variable. In addition, the requirements of (1) time-order, and (2) lack of spuriousness must be met.

(1) Time-Order

In order to establish cause and effect, the dependent variable (the effect) must not occur in time before the onset of the independent variable (the cause). To illustrate: if it can be shown that people who move into neighborhoods with heavy soot-fall *already have* tuberculosis *before* they move there, then we cannot conclude that soot-fall tends to produce tuberculosis. With reference to the relationship between education and prejudice, we would seek to demonstrate that prejudice is reduced *only after* an advanced educational level has been attained.

In some cases, time-order can be simply determined. In regard to the effects of ascriptive characteristics such as sex or race, for example, there can be little question as to the order in which these variables occur since they are present at birth. For many social science propositions, however, it is much more difficult to determine time priority. For instance, does identification with a particular political party lead to the tendency to vote for the candidate of that party? Or, does party identification develop after the vote has been cast? Similarly, does low self-esteem result in criminality?

Or, does the criminal develop low self-esteem as a function of the stigma of criminality? In Chapter 4, we shall discuss a method whereby time-order can be established.

(2) Lack of Spuriousness

Suppose that we find a correlation between soot-fall and tuberculosis and discover that soot-fall preceeds tuberculosis in time. On this basis, can we safely conclude that sootfall contributes to tuberculosis? Not unless we have ruled out the possibility of *spuriousness*. A spurious relationship exists when the association between two variables can be explained by a third variable. In the case of the spurious relationship between sootfall and tuberculosis, the third variable is a dietary deficiency. As a result, the causal proposition might instead focus on the relationship between *diet* and tuberculosis. As another example, consider the proposition, "authoritarian individuals are more prejudice that non-authoritarian individuals." With reference to this relationship, it may turn out to be the case that a third variable such as "status concern" produces both authoritarianism and prejudice. If so, then we could say that the relationship between authoritarianism and prejudice is a spurious relationship.

In order to rule out spuriousness, the researcher must find a way to control for as many relevant third variables as he can. Such methods will be introduced and discussed in Chapter 4.

What is Theory?

Thus far, we have examined the nature of concepts, variables and propositions, the basic elements of theoretical analysis. We now turn our attention to larger questions of *theory*: What is it? What can be done with it? How is it used in the context of social science research?

Like other complex terms, "theory" has been used in several different ways to indicate several different things. Despite this diversity of usages, however, we can identify three widely employed meanings of theory as found in the literature of social science: (1) Theory as Concept, (2) Theory as Conceptual Scheme, and (3) Theory as Consummation of Explanation.

(1) Theory as Concept

Theory is used by many to mean the expression of a concept which represents the nature of social or political reality. In this rather vague and general usage, theory is viewed as "philosophizing" about phenomena of interest to the social scientist, regardless of the particular form that it takes. Thus, we find sociologists addressing themselves to reference group "theory" or to role "theory," though these terms can properly be regarded only as concepts—albeit important concepts—around which a sizable body of research has accumulated.

(2) Theory as Conceptual Scheme

In a more precise meaning, theory is frequently treated as a set of *somewhat* related concepts which represent the nature of social or political reality. In political science, for example, the display of concepts in Figure 3-1 is sometimes regarded as a theory of voter decision making or choice.

Figure 3-1 identifies three concepts and, by means of arrows, indicates that each concept is related to the voter's choice to support one or another of the major political parties. However, this conceptual scheme does not specify *how* each concept is related to voter choice; nor does it specify whether these concepts are related to one another. Instead, it simply indicates that each concept by itself has some influence of an unspecified nature on the individual's voting decision. NOTE: As we shall see below, the scheme in Figure 1 could be given greater explanatory power by clearly specifying the relationships among concepts. For example: The more one identifies with a political party, the greater the probability that one will vote for the candidates of that party.

A second example of "theory as conceptual scheme" can be found in the well-known communication model: "Who says what to whom in which channels with what effect?" (Lasswell, 1960). In this "theory," the important

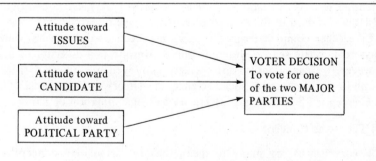

Figure 3-1: A "Theory" of Voter Decision Making.

elements of the process of communication are identified but remain unexplained. That is to say, we are left with a set of "empty boxes" to be filled in by the researcher who seeks to understand the nature of communication. For example, the source of a communication (the "who?" box) might be treated as a variable in the prediction that a highly credible source generates better acceptance of a communication message than does a source having low credibility.

(3) Theory as Consummation of Explanation

To this point, we have defined "theory" with reference to a set of concepts. Unlike previous conceptions, theory as *Consummation of explanation* consists of a set of interrelated propositions, at least one of which is testable by means of research. Any proposition subjected to empirical test is referred to as a *hypothesis* (Phillips, 1971).

Much of the work of social science research is concerned with testing hypotheses about the nature of social or political reality as derived from theory. Some hypotheses are supported by the results of investigation; others are disconfirmed by the data and discarded or revised as needed. Illustrative of some commonly tested social science hypotheses are the following: (1) "The greater the level of frustration, the greater the aggression." (2) "Interpersonal attraction is enhanced to the extent that participants are similar with respect to important values or attitudes." (3) "The more credible or trustworthy the communicator is perceived to be, the greater the tendency to accept his communication." (4) "Those individuals who benefit most from a system of social stratification are most likely to accept it." (5) "The greater the perceived opportunity for upward social mobility, the less radical the political attitude." (6) "The greater the sexual freedom, the less prostitution." (7) "The more decentralized the governmental system, the greater the impact of special interests on policy."

Social scientists typically justify their hypotheses in a loosely structured theoretical rationale which takes the form of a few paragraphs to several pages in which the reasons for their hypothesis are given. At least partial justification for a given hypothesis usually can be found in the existing literature of social science, either in earlier theoretical analyses or in previous research. As a result, the theoretical analysis of a problem almost invariably will include some related literature.

To illustrate, let us consider the hypothesis, "Parent-child attractiveness is enhanced to the extent that they are similar with respect to important values." The theoretical analysis of the foregoing hypothesis might well include (1) earlier theories in which the more general relationship between value consensus (or attitude similarity) and interpersonal attraction has been discussed, and (2) previous research in related areas wherein this relationship has already been tested such as mate selection, friendship choice, and ethnic group relations.

Generating Theory

The intellectual processes involved in generating theory as consummation of explanation can be identified as (1) inductive reasoning and (2) deductive reasoning.

(1) Inductive Reasoning

Inductive reasoning can be conceived as the process of building up from the concrete to the abstract; that is to say, as moving from the base of a pyramid of specific observations and facts to its pinnacle as represented in abstract concepts and propositions. For instance, a student who wishes to study voting behavior examines the voting data in his community. As a result of these observations, he generates a series of questions for which he produces tentative answers in the form of a few systematically related propositions.

As illustrated in Figure 3-2, this reasoning might proceed in the following way: "Most people where I live vote Republican. Why is this so? That is, what characteristic of these people influences them to vote Republican?" Answer: "They are relatively affluent." Assuming that affluence affects voting behavior, Proposition 1 (P1) becomes: Affluent people tend to vote Republican. "Why?" Answer: "Because affluence is a type of reward in the context of industrialized socio-political systems. But why would "rewarded" people vote Republican?" Answer: "Because the Republican Party more than the Democratic Party stands for the status quo." Thus, a more general proposition in terms of which P1 can be incorporated and explained: Individuals rewarded in industrialized socio-political systems tend to support the political group that represents the status quo (P2). "Why is this so?" Answer: "This is a case of self-interest being expressed." If so, an even more general proposition can be derived (P3): In regard to political preference, individuals tend to act in terms of their self-interest.

(2) Deductive Reasoning

As we have seen, the student who uses inductive reasoning proceeds by

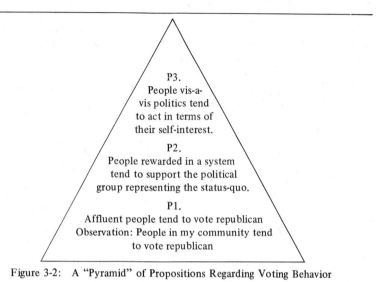

Figure 3-2:   A "Pyramid" of Propositions Regarding Voting Behavior

a continuous chain of questions and answers, beginning at the base of a pyramid consisting of concrete observation and ending with an abstract proposition in which less abstract propositions can be explained. By contrast, *deductive reasoning* starts at the abstract pinnacle of the pyramid in Figure 3-2 and systematically proceeds to its concrete base. In this process, the student initially identifies a general interest or problem, focusing on broad concepts and assumptions. He then moves from this abstract level to derive a set of increasingly more concrete propositions, culminating in at least a single testable hypothesis.

Deductions:

To illustrate: A student might ask, "Is man's political behavior motivated by self-interest?" Answer: "To a large extent, yes. Assuming that man is so motivated (P3), how will he behave when making a voting decision?" Middle-level proposition (P2): Individuals rewarded in industrialized socio-political systems tend to support the political group that represents the status quo. Observations: (1) The Republican party more than the Democratic party stands for the status quo. (2) Affluence is a type of reward in the context of industrialized socio-political systems. Thus, (P1) Affluent people tend to vote Republican.

The Structure of Theory

Social scientists do not always carry out the intellectual processes of induction and deduction to their logical conclusion; nor do they frequently make explicit reference to the nature of the links between their propositions and underlying assumptions. As noted earlier in this chapter, social scientific theories generally take the form of loosely structured rationales in which the reasons for hypotheses are stated, though not as a series of ordered propositions.

Before moving on, however, we should at this juncture examine some of the more systematic forms which theory is capable of taking—forms which are becoming more widely employed by social scientists concerned with increasing their understanding of social or political behavior. The theoretical structures discussed here are (1) the postulate form and (2) the chain form.

(1) The Postulate Form

In the *postulate form* of theory, the investigator assumes or postulates at least one abstract proposition from which more concrete propositions can be derived and tested. By application of logic and appropriate definitions, if the postulate is true, then propositions A, B, C, and D should be true. Moreover, if proposition D is tested and confirmed, the entire theoretical structure including the postulate and untested propositions can be regarded as being more tenable. Consider the following example of the postulate theoretical structure:

Postulate:

Individuals who are rewarded in a system tend to support that system: whereas individuals who go unrewarded tend to reject it.

Proposition A:

The more discrimination by a system against a group, the greater the likelihood that members of that group will resort to rebellion (e.g., riots).

Proposition B:

The more a nation is condemned by an international system (e.g., the United Nations), the stronger the probability that it will reject that system.

Proposition C:

The more a worker is paid by an organization, the more he tends to identify with that organization.

Proposition D:

The greater the affluence, the stronger the tendency to vote.

Proposition E:

The more respect and positive recognition an individual receives from his family, the stronger his identification with that family.

Another example of the postulate form of theory can be found in the well known study of suicide by Durkheim (1951). A basic postulate in Durkheim's theory is that "the greater the integration of a group, the less suicide within that group." From this assumption, it is possible to derive numerous testable hypotheses which predict for example that suicide is more likely (A) among Protestants than among Catholics, (B) among the single, divorced, and widowed than among the married, (C) among children of broken homes than among children of stable homes, and (D) among city dwellers than among rural dwellers.

(2) The Chain Form

As a chain connects its component parts, so a theory in *chain form* links a set of propositions by means of shared variables. From this structure, it is possible to derive an additional but limited set of propositions, any of which might be tested by the researcher. Confirmation of a derived proposition has implications for the entire theory including other derived as well as original propositions.

To illustrate this form of theory, consider the following "chain" of propositions having to do with the so-called "Democratic dilemma of developing countries":

A) The more a political system stresses equalitarianism, the more civic participation is valued.

B) The more civic participation is valued, the greater the civic participation.

C) The greater the civic participation, the greater the demand for short-term rewards.

D) The greater the demand for short-term rewards, the greater the allocation of system resources for consumer items.

E) The greater the allocation for consumer items, the less ability for long-range economic development.

Deductions:

A) The more a political system stresses equalitarianism, (1) the greater the civic participation, (2) the greater the demand for short-term rewards, (3) the greater the allocation of system resources for consumer items, (4) the less ability for long-range economic development.

B) The more civic participation is valued, (1) the greater the demand for short-term rewards, (2) the greater the allocation of system resources for consumer items, (3) the less ability for long-range economic development.

C) The greater the civic participation, (1) the greater the allocation of system resources for consumer items, (2) the less ability for long-range economic development.

D) The greater the demand for short-term rewards, (1) the less ability for long-range economic development.

As shown in the foregoing example, five interrelated propositions produce 10 testable deductions. By tradition, the derived proposition which relates the first and last variables of the original set of propositions (in this case, Deduction A4) is tested.

It should be noted that other variations of this basic chain form of theory are possible. For instance, the theoretical structure known as a *model* is held together by a common factor, the dependent variable. However, the independent variables of a model may be separately related to its dependent variable by means of chain-like substructures which specify the linkages in the causal relationship. Detailed discussion of theoretical models lies beyond the scope of this book.

Evaluation of Theory

How can a theory be evaluated? Having conducted a theoretical analysis, on what basis do we decide whether it is worthwhile or ineffective? The following general criteria are frequently applied for this purpose: (1) explanation (and prediction), (2) scope, (3) parsimony, and (4) fruitfulness.

(1) Explanation (and Prediction)

An effective theory is capable of *explaining* social or political phenomena. In connection with social science research, explanation has two important meanings. In the first place, to explain is to increase our *understanding* of the causes of a phenomenon under investigation. This means that the answers generated by a theory are tentatively accepted based upon the rationale of the theory by a community of social scientists who seek to better understand a phenomenon. In its second meaning, explanation refers to the *empirical test* of a hypothesis. If a hypothesis is supported by the results of research, the underlying theory is said to explain some part of the data. If, however, a hypothesis is disconfirmed, then the theory is not regarded as an effective explanation.

The ability of the social scientist to accurately predict the occurrence of an event is related to this second meaning of explanation—that meaning which depends upon the empirical test of a hypothesis. For instance, if a theory indicates that frustration produces increased aggression, it should be possible to predict the level of aggression from observing the level of frustration (assuming, of course, that other relevant variables have been controlled). Moreover, in the context of a laboratory experiment, it should be possible to *create* aggressive behavior by manipulating the level of frustration experienced by the subjects. In this way, we explain the occurrence of aggression.

It should be noted that the explanatory power of social scientific theories is relatively weak especially in terms of prediction. At best, present-day theories account for slight differences in behavior. As social scientific explanations develop, however, we should be able to increase the accuracy of our predictions as well.

(2) Scope

What happens when competing theories predict the same outcome? In such cases, *scope* or level of generality becomes an important criterion for choosing between them. It was earlier noted that abstract concepts tend to be more useful than their concrete counterparts. In a similar way, we can now suggest that theories which explain a larger number of phenomena— that have greater scope—are more effective theories. The reason is clear: the researcher who uses an abstract theory gets more for his effort, in so far as he explains a wider range of phenomena. It is something like the fisherman who uses a fishing rod to catch fish, when he could have used a large net. The result is greater output for the same expenditure of effort.

(3) Parsimony

Any theory may be evaluated with respect to *parsimony*. A parismonious theory is a simple theory; it employs a small number of assumptions and propositions in order to explain a given phenomenon. Holding other considerations constant, the simpler theory is always preferable to the more complex theory. For example, a theory in which juvenile delinquency is explained with three independent variables may be superior to a theory which explains juvenile delinquency with ten independent variables.

(4) Fruitfulness

To the list of criteria for judging the effectiveness of theory including explanation, scope, and parsimony, we must add a final item. This criterion, *fruitfulness*, refers to the capacity of theory to generate new inquiries and discoveries.

> Suppose for example, that our efforts to explain the rules of international law lead ... to the theory that, by and large, the influence of a state ... rests on two factors (1) its reputed or actual ability to impose its desires through coercive measures, and (2) its reputed or actual willingness to employ such measures. In other words, international law is a function of the relative power and interest of the states concerned. The very enunciation of the theory leads to questions concerning circumstances in which it does or does not hold true ... [and] even more, suggests questions and hypotheses concerning the factors shaping the development of law within countries. If international law reflects a combination of power and interest, what of assumption that domestic law reflects the common good or the public interest or justice? ... that government ... constitutes a sort of impartial arbiter serving to 'adjust' conflicting claims ... (Van Dyke, 1960, pp. 107–108).

One of the more fruitful theories in social science can be found in Festinger's (1957) Theory of Cognitive Dissonance, according to which making a decision per se creates dissonance ("nonfitting relations" among cognitions) as well as the pressure to reduce dissonance. Despite its essentially social psychological nature, this theory has been applied to explain such diverse phenomena as race relations in the United States, the onset of rumors in the aftermath of a disaster, and reactions to disconfirmation among true believers, to mention just a few. The many hundreds of studies which have been devised in order to test or examine the implications of the theory of Cognitive Dissonance attest to its unusual fruitfulness. In such research, a variety of relevant questions and answers beyond the original focus of the theory have been generated, the ultimate result being greater output for an initial research investment.

What's Ahead

In Chapter 3, we have examined the nature of theoretical analysis, including its key elements of concepts, variables, propositions, and theory. Once the researcher has conducted a theoretical analysis, his next step usually takes the form of developing a strategy for collecting data and testing at least one of the hypotheses that can be derived from a theory. The purpose of the next chapter is to provide some important guidelines for the data collection process.

Exercises

1) State a social science theory (theory as consummation of explanation), identifying its major elements—its concepts, independent and dependent variables, and propositions—and at least one testable hypothesis.

2) Explain how you might go about operationally defining the key concepts in the theory stated in Exercise #1.

3) On the basis of criteria presented in Chapter 3, evaluate the probable effectiveness of the social science theory stated in Exercise #1.

4) From your knowledge of social science, select an appropriate example to represent each of the three conceptions of theory presented in Chapter 3: theory as concept, theory as conceptual scheme, and theory as consummation of explanation.

5) Taking into account the range of intellectual processes and theoretical forms available to the social scientist, generate your own theory (as consummation of explanation) and at least one testable hypothesis for any problem in social science.

CHAPTER 4:   COLLECTING THE DATA

We are continually collecting data about the world around us, though generally in an informal and haphazard manner. It happens each and every time we make an observation: whenever we witness the behavior of our associates at work or our children at play; when we ask friends how they intend to vote in an election; when we read a magazine or watch television.

The basic difference between our everyday methods of data collection and those of the social scientist is a matter of degree rather than kind. The social scientist who conducts research—to a much greater extent than most of us—makes his observations in a systematic way, so as to maximize efficiency and minimize the possibility that personal bias or misconception will interfere with his objectivity.

To test his hypotheses, the social scientist must select an appropriate method for gathering the data. In the present chapter, some of the most useful of these methods for student research—experiments, surveys, content analysis, and secondary analysis—are defined and illustrated. We begin with a discussion of the experiment.

The Basic Experiment

The most important distinguishing characteristic of an *experiment* is that the researcher systematically manipulates one or more of the independent variables to which his subjects are exposed. By manipulation, we mean that he assigns the independent variable to one group of individuals but withholds it from another group of individuals. The group that receives the independent variable (or *treatment*) is known as an *experimental group*; the group that does not receive the independent variable is called a *control group*.

To illustrate: an experimenter who seeks to test the hypothesis that frustration increases prejudice might manipulate frustration by giving a difficult (or *frustrating*) examination to the members of an experimental group, while the members of a control group are permitted to relax or to take a much easier version of the same examination. If a subsequent measure reveals greater prejudice in the experimental group than in the control group, then this difference is attributed to the independent variable, frustration. Similarly, a researcher testing the effect of source credibility on attitude toward socialized medicine might manipulate the credibility of a communicator by informing the experimental group that the communicator is a well-known medical scholar (high credibility), while identifying the same communicator to the control group as an obscure student (low credibility). If credibility really influences attitude toward socialized medicine, then members of the experimental group should agree more with the communicator than members of the control group.

Experiments can be conducted in either (1) an after-only or (2) a before-after arrangement, depending upon when the dependent variable is measured. In either case, the researcher's objective is to create a controlled situation in which the influence of an independent variable on a dependent variable can be directly observed.

(1) The After-Only Design

As illustrated in Figure 4-1, the basic *after-only experimental design* consists of two groups of subjects, an experimental group (E) and a control group (C) whose members are given a measure of the dependent variable in a *posttest* session, that is, *only after* the independent variable has been manipulated. Thus, prejudice is measured for the members of E and C only after the frustrating treatment has been given out. Likewise, the attitudes of members of E and C are recorded only after the credibility of a communicator has been varied.

GROUP:	*E*	*C*
TREATMENT:	Frustration	No Frustration
POSTTEST:	Measure of Prejudice	Measure of Prejudice

Figure 4-1: An after-only experimental design for a study of the effect of frustration on prejudice.

The experimenter usually seeks to establish a difference between the posttests of his experimental and control groups—a group difference that can be attributed to the independent variable he has manipulated rather than to the myriad extraneous factors that may influence human behavior. With reference to the hypothesis that frustration increases prejudice, for example, he hopes to find greater prejudice among members of E (those who were exposed to the frustrating treatment) than among members of C (those who were not similarly exposed). If such a difference occurs, it is attributed to the effect of the independent variable.

But how do we rule out the possibility of spuriousness? How do we know that the difference between E and C might not be the product of some uncontrolled third variable? Suppose, for instance, that members of the experimental group (but not members of the control group)—prior to being exposed to the experimental frustration—unknowingly attended a meeting of the Ku Klux Klan or viewed an anti-Semitic film. Either experience might affect the overall level of prejudice in the group. What can be done so that causality is not falsely assigned to our independent variable?

Ideally, we seek the assurance that our independent variable—the experimental treatment—is the *one* and *only* difference distinguishing the experimental group from the control group. If, for example, the members of E were exposed to an anti-Semitic film, we should like to be sure that members of C were similarly exposed. To This end, we might reasonably consider *matching* the members of E and C with respect to possible independent variables.

For the sake of illustration, let us return to a hypothetical study to determine the effect of source credibility on attitude toward socialized medicine. Suppose, in this connection, that the members of the experimental and control groups all heard the same lecture in favor of socialized medicine. To members of the experimental group, the lecturer was introduced as Dr. Thomas Johnson, a well-known expert in his field (high credibility); to members of the control group, however, the same lecturer was identified as Tom Johnson, a freshman biology major at a local college (low credibility). Let us also say that a posttest measure of attitude toward socialized medicine revealed that the members of E (high credibility) were more in agreement with the lecturer's position regarding socialized medicine than were members of C (low credibility).

It may well be the case, of course, that the independent variable in the foregoing example, source credibility, actually brought members of the experimental group in closer agreement with the lecturer who favored socialized medicine. This is the hoped for result. It can also be argued, however, that members of the experimental group may have initially differed from members of the control group in some important yet unknown ways—ways that could influence their attitudes toward socialized medicine. Imagine, for example, that a disproportionately large number of the members of the experimental group previously experienced a costly illness for which they could not pay. Or, suppose members of the control group tended to be politically more conservative than members of the experimental group. Despite an obtained difference between E and C, it might still be contended therefore that source credibility really has had no influence on attitudes toward socialized medicine, since such a difference might have been present before the experiment began.

To rule out spuriousness, we might decide to *match* our subjects from the experimental and control groups with respect to such relevant characteristics as socio-economic status or political orientation. In so doing, we would make sure that the same number of conservative and liberal subjects from similar socio-economic positions were included in each group. To take another example: if we were studying the effect of teaching methods on rate of learning, we might consider matching our subjects in regard to IQ, grade-point-average, socio-economic status, as well as on any other variable that might have an impact on learning.

Matching members of experimental and control groups can be an effective way to minimizie the possibility of spuriousness. But it sometimes creates more problems than it solves. For one thing, matching—especially subject-by-subject matching—tends to reduce the number of acceptable subjects to an absurd extent. To end up with 100 subjects who have been matched on a few "key" variables such as IQ and grade-point-average may require beginning with an initial pool of at least several hundred potential subjects, most of whom are discarded in the process of getting the ultimate sample (for example, if we have a member of the experimental group with a 2.4 grade-point-average whose IQ is 122, then we must find a similar subject for our control group).

As we have seen, then, the demands of matching may for some purposes be impractical to achieve. Moreover, matching does not always provide the assurance that experimental and control groups are equivalent. How can we possibly know *all* of the key variables on which to match our subjects? For instance, despite a laborious effort to achieve matched groups in terms of IQ and grade-point-average, we might later find a difference between E and C with respect to level of motivation or previous training in the subject—a difference that could easily account for differential rates of learning.

Given the foregoing limitations associated with matching, how is it possible to obtain comparable experimental and control groups? The answer lies in the nature of *randomization*, the procedure whereby subjects are assigned on a random basis to the experimental and control conditions, so that E and C differ by chance alone. With the aid of randomization, we can for all practical purposes rule out the factor of spuriousness: if a difference results between our experimental and control groups, we can be relatively sure—on a probability basis—that our manipulated independent variable is the causal agent.

Randomization can be carried out by putting the name of every subject on a separate slip of paper and, while blindfolded, drawing names for the experimental and control groups from a hat. For example, if 100 names are to be assigned, the first 50 subjects drawn from a hat might go into the experimental group whereas the second 50 subjects might be placed into the control group. In this way, if some of the experimental group subjects have seen an anti-Semitic film, we can assume that some of the control group subjects have seen it too. Likewise, if conservative and upper-class subjects are represented in the experimental group, we assume that similar subjects can be found in the control group.

Randomization can be carried out without the aid of blindfold and hat. A simple alternative would be to assign subjects to experimental and control groups by the flip of a coin ("heads"=E; "tails"=C). Or, in the case of a group-administered treatment (for example, the written version of a speech whose source is to be varied), the experimenter might shuffle together the experimental and control conditions (for example, high credibility versus low credibility) and hand them out in sequence.

In sum: the after-only experimental design can be regarded as a powerful method for establishing causality. In conjunction with randomization, it can be used to establish association between an independent variable and a dependent variable. Moreover, since the researcher actually carries out a manipulation, he can also be sure that the independent variable occurs in time before the dependent variable. Finally, by means of matching or randomization, he can minimize the possibility of spuriousness or rule it out altogether.

(2) The Before-After Design

As we have seen, the after-only experimental design involves measuring a dependent variable just once—after the independent variable has been manipulated. For most student projects of an experimental nature, this design works well in regard to establishing causality. Before leaving the topic of basic experimental design, however, we must consider an alternative experimental arrangement which also has a good deal of popularity especially among experimentalists who are concerned with the study of change. Known as the *before-after design*, this approach requires measuring the dependent variable *both* before and after the independent variable has been manipulated.

In the one-group version of the before-after design as illustrated in Figure 4-2, we make the assumption that the experimental group "serves as its own control." That is to say, any difference obtained between the posttest measures of the dependent variable is attributed to the independent variable. If, for example, the overall level of prejudice increases from pretest to posttest, we assume that the treatment which intervened, our frustrating treatment, is responsible.

Despite its appealing simplicity, the one-group before-after design in generally not recommended, especially if a more effective alternative can be applied. This is because the one-group version fails to provide adequate controls for spuriousness. With reference to the effect of frustration on prejudice, for instance, we cannot be certain that pretest-posttest increase in prejudice would have occurred regardless of the presence of frustration. In this connection, suppose that, during the interval separating the pretest from the posttest, subjects are exposed to an anti-Semitic film which heightens their prejudices. Or, in a long-term study of children, prejudice might increase as a function of their internalization of parental prejudices over many years. In the one-group version of a before-after design, we have no way to determine whether an obtained increase in prejudice from the pretest to the posttest occurs as a result of our independent variable, frustration, or as a result of some uncontrolled factor such as aging or viewing an anti-Semitic film.

A much more effective experimental arrangement can be found in the

GROUP:	*E*
PRETEST:	Measure of Prejudice
TREATMENT:	Frustration
POSTTEST:	Measure of Prejudice

Figure 4-2:   A one-group before-after experimental design for a study of the effect of frustration on prejudice.

GROUP:	E	C
PRETEST:	Measure of Prejudice	Measure of Prejudice
TREATMENT:	Frustration	Frustration
POSTTEST:	Measure of Prejudice	Measure of Prejudice

Figure 4-3:   A two-group before-after experimental design for a study of the effect of frustration on prejudice.

two-group version of the before-after design. As shown in Figure 4-3, this design consists of an experimental group whose members receive the independent variable and a control group whose members do not receive it. Pretest and posttest measures of the dependent variable are taken for both groups.

By the addition of a control group, the two group design controls for many sources of spuriousness, since whatever extraneous factors are at work among members of the experimental group can usually be assumed to operate among members of the control group as well. Moreover, the presence of a pretest permits making precise comparisons in regard to change in the dependent variable—comparisons that are not possible for the researcher who employs an after-only design.

To illustrate: if maturational change (that is, aging) occurs in the experimental group, then the same maturational change can be assumed to operate in the control group (i.e., they grow older too). If an anti-Semitic film is available to members of the experimental group, then it is also available to members of the control group. Since such extraneous factors are equalized between groups, we can assume that an obtained difference in the dependent variable is a function of our manipulated independent variable.

More Complex Experiments

A basic experimental design—either after-only or before-after—can be extended to incorporate (1) a larger number of categories of the independent variable under investigation or (2) a larger number of independent variables. In either case, the researcher who extends the complexity of his experimental design is attempting to better approximate the nature of the "real world" phenomena that he ultimately seeks to explain. For example, a researcher who studies the effect of frustration on prejudice may decide that the "all or none" approach represented by "frustration" versus "no frustration" is unnecessarily imprecise, since frustrations in real life are a matter of degree. As a result, he may add a category to his independent variable, thereby creating the experimental conditions—severe frustration (E_1), mild frustration (E_2), and no frustration (C)—as illustrated in Figure 4-4. This could be done by adding an experimental group to the basic design as follows: giving an extremely difficult examination to E_1, a somewhat difficult examination to E_2, and an easy examination to C.

Another way to introduce "real-world" characteristics into a basic experimental design is to study more than one independent variable at a time. This has the two-fold advantage of (1) permitting the simultaneous investigation of two or more independent variables; an important consideration if subjects are hard to obtain, and (2) providing the opportunity to study *interactions* between independent variables. The concept of "interaction" indicates that two or more independent variables can combine to produce effects not achieved with either independent variable by itself. It is analogous to the situation of a chemist who combines two or more seemingly innocuous chemicals in order to produce a powerful explosion. In a similar way, the independent variables in social science often interact to yield effects of a different order or intensity. For example, frustration may increase prejudice, but only among authoritarian subjects. Or, frustration may increase prejudice overall, but significantly more so among high authoritarians than among their low-authoritarian counterparts. In either case, we have two independent variables, level of frustration (frustration versus no frustration) and authoritarianism of subject (high versus low). As illustrated in figure 4-5, an experiment in which these two independent variables are simultaneously examined would permit all possible combinations of their categories, thus creating 4 groups of subjects: Frustration/

GROUP:	E_1	E_2	C
TREATMENT:	Severe Frustration	Mild Frustration	No Frustration
POSTTEST:	Measure of Prejudice	Measure of Prejudice	Measure of Prejudice

Figure 4-4: A three-group after-only experimental design for a study of the effect of frustration on prejudice.

LEVEL OF FRUSTRATION:	Frustration		No Frustration	
AUTHORITARIANISM:	High	Low	High	Low
GROUP #	1	2	3	4

Figure 4-5:   An experimental design for the study of the joint influence of frustration and authoritarianism on prejudice.

High Authoritarian, Frustration/Low Authoritarian, No Frustration/High Authoritarian, and No Frustration/Low Authoritarian.

We might increase the complexity of the foregoing experimental design by adding a third independent variable. For example, suppose we hypothesized that frustration produces greater prejudice among high authoritarian subjects than among low authoritarian subjects, but only when the target of prejudice has been presented as weak or particularly vulnerable. (Authoritarian individuals tend to despise weakness and glorify the powerful). As shown in Figure 4-6 (see page 41), an experiment in which the foregoing hypothesis could be tested would generate 8 groups of subjects.

The Survey

As we have seen, the experimenter actually has a direct hand in creating the effect that he seeks to achieve. The manipulation of an independent variable is an essential characteristic of experimental research. By contrast, survey research can be regarded as *retrospective,* in that the effects of independent variables on dependent variables are *recorded* (but not manipulated) after—and sometimes long after—they have occurred.

Forms of Survey Research

Survey research can be cross-sectional or longitudinal in form. In the case of a *cross-sectional* survey, data are collected by comparing a set of individuals or groups at a single point in time. In the language of experimental design, the cross-sectional survey consists of giving the post-test measure of the dependent variable to members of the "experimental" and "control" groups, even though no experimental treatment has been administered. To illustrate, in order to study the relationship between frustration and prejudice, we might compare the degree of prejudice of two groups of respondents: those who have led extremely frustrating lives and those who have not experienced much frustration. Frustration might be indicated by (1) the presence of a physical handicap, (2) social isolation, (3) low socio-economic status, or (4) poor grade-point-average. In a similar way, to investigate "centralism," the centralization or concentration of governmental power at the state level, as related to state spending, we might compare states high and low in centralism in terms of their per capita expenditures.

The *longitudinal* form of a survey proceeds by comparing a single group or set of individuals at different points in time. In the language of experimental research, it consists of giving pretest and posttest measures of the dependent variable to members of an "experimental" group, though no experimental treatment has been administered by the investigator.

For example, the relationship between frustration and prejudice might be investigated by examining a number of individuals over an extended period, so that changes in their level of frustration and prejudice can be measured on a yearly basis. Similarly, the link between centralism and state spending might be studied by examining a single state (for example, the state of Illinois) for a length of time, noting changes that occur in spending and centralism over the course of that period.

In order to conduct a longitudinal survey, the researcher must obtain the same respondents at different points in time. To the extent that longitudinal data are difficult to collect in the context of a short-term project, the longitudinal survey is not usually recommended for the purpose of carrying out student research. It is possible, however, for the student who conducts a cross-sectional survey to incorporate certain characteristics of a longitudinal approach by conducting a *retrospective pretest* in which respondents are asked to recall their attitudes or behavior at an earlier point in time as well as the present. For example, to study the effect of nursery school experiences on the mother-child relationship, we might ask each mother to

LEVEL OF FRUSTRATION:	Frustration				No Frustration			
AUTHORITARIANISM	High		Low		High		Low	
STRENGTH OF TARGET	weak	strong	weak	strong	weak	strong	weak	strong
GROUP #	1	2	3	4	5	6	7	8

Figure 4-6: An experimental design for the study of the joint influence of frustration, authoritarianism, and strength of target on prejudice.

indicate for "now" as well as "before your child entered this nursery school" to what extent she permitted her child to play with household items classified as dangerous or messy. In this way, a "before-after" comparison can be made, though data are collected at only one point in time.

Questionnaires and Interviews

The survey researcher who hopes to reconstruct causal relationships—relationships that have taken place before the study begins—usually has to rely upon the verbal reports of his respondents. These reports can be elicited by means of self-administered questionnaires or in face-to-face interviews.

As compared with the interview, the self-administered *questionnaire* has the distinct advantage that a respondent's anonymity can be better assured. To the extent that sensitive or threatening issues are involved, a respondent may feel more comfortable if he is permitted to answer questions privately than in the presence of an interviewer. In turn, this may well affect the frankness with which a respondent is willing to reply.

Moreover, since the presence of a trained interviewer is not required, the questionnaire is relatively inexpensive to administer. It can be sent by mail or group administered to a large number of respondents at the same time. However, this advantage of the questionnaire also contains a built-in weakness; namely, the questionnaire requires an educational level that many respondents may not have attained. By contrast, an interviewer can clarify ambiguous questions and probe for a detailed answer, so that the understanding of each respondent is maximized, regardless of his intellectual sophistication or level of formal education.

The form of an interview can vary widely according to the particular objectives of a researcher. In seeking to conduct a preliminary study of a previously unexplored topic, he may choose a *nondirective* approach in which questions are constructed as an interview proceeds and new insights about the topic are gained. If, however, the researcher's objective is to test hypotheses in a systematic way, he will more likely decide in favor of an *interview schedule* which contains a predetermined list of questions to which a respondent is asked to reply.

The Nature of Survey Questions

Having chosen among alternative strategies for conducting a survey, the researcher must come up with a series of specific questions with which he can effectively get the data and test his hypotheses. This generally involves a choice between open and closed ended questions, depending upon the particular needs of the survey.

An *open-ended* question raises an issue but allows the respondent to answer in his own terms, without restricting him to predetermined response alternatives. As a result, the open-ended question may be especially appropriate for exploratory studies undertaken for the purpose of generating (as opposed to testing) hypotheses—studies in which the researcher cannot anticipate the nature of the responses he is likely to secure.

Suppose, for example, that we ask students how they feel about a proposed student strike. With the aid of an open-ended question such as,

---

HOW DO YOU FEEL ABOUT THE
UPCOMING STUDENT STRIKE?

---

we might begin to uncover the separate dimensions to which student attitudes are related. We might find, for instance, that many students give political reasons for their support or nonsupport of the strike, whereas a few might indicate feelings of intimidation by their fellow students or might express an underlying need to identify with a cause, regardless of its nature.

The open-ended question generates the widest possible range of responses. By contrast, the *closed-ended question* limits the respondent to a choice among specific alternatives. As a result, the closed-ended question is simpler to use and less time consuming to analyze. Moreover, the closed-ended question better assures the researcher of getting responses along the single dimension that he seeks (for example, in the sample question above, political attitudes toward the student strike).

The advantages of closed-ended questions can be illustrated with reference to the situation in which demographic information such as sex, marital status, and income are to be obtained. As shown below, such closed-ended items are easily interpreted by a wide range of respondents. Moreover, by the procedure of *precoding*, a set of response categories can be assigned numerical values (for instance, 1, 2, 3 and 4) in the data collection phase of study. As we shall see in subsequent chapters, this procedure usually facilitates the analysis of data, especially if statistics and/or electronic data processing are to be employed.

Consider the following closed-ended questions:

Your sex: (check one and only one)
    1_____Male
    2_____Female
Your marital status: (check one and only one)
    1_____Married
    2_____Single
    3_____Widowed
    4_____Divorced
Your total annual income from all sources: (check one and only one)
    1_____$2000 or less
    2_____$2001–$5000
    3_____$5001–7000
    4_____$7001–10,000
    5_____$10,001–15000
    6_____$15001–or more

Important theoretical questions can often be cast in a closed-ended format. For example, the concept of "subjective social class" is measured by asking the respondent,

---

In which of the following classes do you belong? (check one and only one)
    1_____Upper
    2_____Middle
    3_____Working
    4_____Lower

To measure family size, we might ask,

How many children do you have? (circle one of the following)
0 1 2 3 4 5 6 7 8 9 or more

Use of marijuana can be examined and compared by asking.

How often have you used marijuana in the last month? (check one and only one)

1_____Very often
2_____Sometimes
3_____Rarely
4_____Not at all

Attitudes toward Puerto Ricans can be inferred by asking respondents to "place an "X" in one position between the adjectives of each scale (e.g., _____: ___X___:_____) to indicate how well these adjectives apply in general to Puerto Ricans."

PUERTO RICANS

kind____:____:____:____:____:____:____ cruel
      1   2   3   4   5   6   7

good____:____:____:____:____:____:____ bad
      1   2   3   4   5   6   7

clean____:____:____:____:____:____:____ dirty
      1   2   3   4   5   6   7

In addition to the many closed-ended items that can be constructed for the particular needs of a given research project, numerous scales—previously developed by other social science researchers—are presently available for the use of the student researcher. Existing measures include alienation, anomie, neighborliness, community participation, ethnocentrism, socioeconomic status, attitude toward work, traditional family ideology, status concern, authoritarianism, and political orientation, to mention only a few. These scales are located in social science journals and in several books containing large collections of such measures.[*]

It should be noted also that closed and open-ended questions can be used in combination as well as separately. An effective way to learn the "reasons" associated with a particular response is to lead with a closed-

---

[*] See, for example, Bonjean, (1967) and Robinson, Rusk and Head (1968).

ended item and follow with an open-ended "Why?" question. For example, the following combination of questions can be used to investigate students' career plans and the reasons associated with them:

A) Thinking of your career plans, which of the following broad occupational areas would you most like to enter? (check one and only one)

1_____Business-Industry
2_____Government
3_____Education
4_____Other non-profit social service
5_____other_____
     (specify)

B) Why do you say that?

The Art of Asking Questions

It is possible to summarize some of the important points related to construction and application of questions for interview schedules and questionnaires.

1) *Avoid "loaded" questions.* Questions should be phrased so that the respondent does not feel he is being coerced to respond in any particular way. For example, the researcher who uses the question, "Most people in our town identify with the Republican party—Do you?" would be unfairly "loading" the question to produce an affirmative response.

2) *Ask relevant questions.* Questions must provide the information necessary

to test the researcher's hypotheses. In this regard, students may construct their questionnaires or interview schedules without properly evaluating the appropriateness of items for answering the questions with which their study began. For example, if the relationship between frustration and prejudice is to be investigated, then at least some of the questions must focus upon these variables. This is not to say, however, that *all* questions must be related to explicit hypotheses. On the contrary, interesting findings can be obtained and new hypotheses generated by analyzing questions only tangentially related to the researcher's initial questions. The rule of relevance should be applied with sensitivity and discretion.

3) *Place sensitive or threatening questions last.* The placement of questions must yield a sense of continuity, permitting an interviewer (or respondent) to move easily from one question to the next. For this reason, questions may be grouped together on the basis of their common subject matter or because they focus upon activities occurring at the same point in time or space. However, an even more important issue related to the order of questions has to do with the senstivity or threat associated with questionnaires and interview schedules. For example, many respondents are reluctant to give their income or age, nor do they care to discuss their sexual relations with strange interviewers. Individuals are usually most resistant to such controversial or "personal" items in the initial phase of the interview or questionnaire, when they are still very much on their guard. It is therefore advisable in general to place the most innocuous or easiest questions at the beginning and the most threatening or difficult items toward the end.

4) *Maintain a careful balance between distance and friendliness.* This suggestion applies only to the interview situation. A cool and distant interviewer may unintentionally discourage the cooperation of his respondents; producing a high rate of refusal to participate as well as unnecessarily brief responses once participation is secured.

At the opposite extreme, an inordinately friendly interviewer may obtain unnecessarily lengthy interviews (especially with socially isolated respondents) and systematically distorted responses. In this connection, respondents often try to please the "pleasant" interviewer by answering questions as they perceive the interviewer *wants* to hear them answered. The interviewer can minimize this effect by attempting to maintain a balance between distance and friendliness; a result that can be achieved with careful training in the use of the schedule before interviewing actually begins.

Sampling Methods

To this point, we have pretended that the survey researcher actually studies the entire population of individuals he seeks to understand. In the present context, a *population* refers to a set of individuals who share at least one characteristic, whether membership in a voluntary association, common citizenship, ethnicity, school enrollment, or the like. In point of fact, surveys are rarely taken of each and every member of a given population. By virtue of his limited resources, the survey researcher typically studies only a *sample*, a smaller number of individuals who are in some way representative of the population. Through the process of sampling, he attempts to generalize from his sample (the small group) to the entire population from which the sample was drawn (the large group).

How does the researcher go about the task of drawing a sample that is representative of the population in which he has an interest? The selection is made on the basis that each and every member of the population can be given an equal chance of being drawn into the sample. If such a requirement is met, then the researcher uses a random sampling method; otherwise, he employs a non-random sampling method.

(1) Non-Random Samples

The most popular non-random sampling method. *accidental sampling*, is based exclusively on what is convenient for the researcher. He includes the most accessible cases from the population (and excludes the inconvenient cases). An example of accidental sampling would be for a student researcher to administer a questionnaire to all of the students enrolled in a course he is presently taking.

Another non-random approach to sampling can be found in the *quota sample*, whereby diverse characteristics of a population such as age, social class, or ethnicity, are sampled in the proportions which they occupy in the population. If, for example, a student researcher wishes to draw a quota sample of the students attending a particular university, he might employ the following procedure: (1) pinpoint a relevant characteristic and its proportions in the population of students (for example, 41 percent of the students are females and 59 percent are males); and (2) give interviewers a quota of students to locate (in this case, so that only 41 percent of the sample consists of females and 59 percent consists of males).

A final variation of the non-random approach is known as *judgment sampling*. By this method, "logic" or "commonsense" is used as the basis for selecting a sample that is representative of a larger population. To illustrate, a student who seeks to draw a sample of university students might on an intuitive basis decide to interview students in dormitories, the library, and the cafeteria, since these places are habituated by diverse campus groups.

(2) Random Samples

Accidental, quota, and judgment samples are relatively easy and inexpensive to construct, but often yield only rough estimates of population characteristics. This is especially true of accidental sampling. By contrast, *random samples* by virtue of the fact that they give each and every member of the population an equal chance of being selected for the sample tend to have much greater accuracy with respect to representing population characteristics.

In order to consider each and every population member, it is usually necessary that we come up with a complete list of population members. For instance, a student researcher who seeks to study fellow students enrolled in his college might ask the registrar for the official list of students. From such a list, a small sample of students could be chosen at random for the purpose of interviewing or answering a questionnaire.

One of the simplest and most effective procedures for randomly selecting sample members from a list can be found in *systematic random sampling*, whereby a list of population members is sampled by fixed intervals. That is to say, the decision is made to include every *nth* member of a population in the ultimate sample. To illustrate, in order to draw a random sample from an entire population of 10,000 college students, we might secure a list of students from the registrar's office, take every 100th name on the list, and come up with a sample of 100 students who represent the entire student body.

Random sampling can sometimes be made more effective by the procedures of stratifying or clustering.

Stratifying involves dividing the population into more homogeneous subgroups or *strata* from which the random samples are then taken. Suppose, for example, we wish to study race differences in regard to attitudes toward the police among the students, both black and white, at a particular university. To the extent that attitudes toward the police vary by race, stratification by race (for example, black versus white) would form more homogeneous subgroups with respect to the acceptance of the police. The researcher would proceed to take a random sample (for example, every nth individual) from each racial group.

Stratification has at least two advantages: (1) It requires a smaller sample size to yield the same degree of accuracy, since homogeneous groups require smaller samples than do heterogeneous groups; and (2) It can be useful for conducting a more intensive analysis of a subgroup or stratum which contains few cases. In the foregoing study, for instance, it might be considered desirable to conduct a detailed analysis of the relatively few black students enrolled in this particular college. By means of stratification, it would be possible to take a disproportionately large number of black students, so that this analysis could be carried out.

Clustering is widely employed to reduce the costs of large surveys in which interviewers must be sent to scattered localities and traveling is required. With this method, sampling proceeds at two levels: (1) at the level of the *primary sampling unit* or cluster—some rather well delineated area which can be regarded as including characteristics found in the entire population (For example, a state, census tract, city block, or classroom), and (2) at the level of the sample members within each cluster.

For illustrative purposes, suppose we wish to interview a representative sample of students living on-campus at a large university. Treating the dormitory as our primary sampling unit or cluster, we might proceed by securing a list of all dormitories at the university, from which we draw a random sample of such dormitories (for example, by taking every nth dormitory). Having drawn this sample of dormitories, we could then select the individual students in each dormitory by the same random method (for example, take every nth student in each of the selected dormitories).

Content Analysis

Up to this point, we have discussed methods of data collection which usually require securing the cooperation of a set of respondents—respondents whose awareness of being measured may actually affect the nature of their responses. For instance, the act of taking an experimental pretest might have an impact on the respondent's attitude or learning which we falsely attribute to the treatment being manipulated. In a related way, survey respondents may attempt to please an interviewer by responding in the direction perceived as being requested, rather than by giving an honest answer.

In response to such problems associated with surveys and experiments, it is possible to employ a set of "unobtrusive" or nonreactive methods of data collection: methods not requiring the conscious participation of a set of respondents or subjects. Here are some examples of unobtrusive methods:

1) An investigator can count empty bottles in trashcans, in order to determine the level of liquor consumption in a town that is legally "dry" (Webb, et al., 1966).

2) The rate at which floor tiles erode and are replaced can be used to indicate the relative popularity of museum exhibits (Webb et al, 1966).

3) "Lost letters" in stamped envelopes bearing addresses such as American Communist Party or John Birch Society can be dropped around public mailboxes; the rate at which they are mailed by passersby being used as a measure of community support for the group or individual to whom they are addressed (Webb, 1966).

The unobtrusive method known as *content analysis* has taken on increasing importance as an approach to the conduct of social science research.* By this method, a researcher asks questions of the communication messages that people have previously produced, and, in so doing, seeks to objectively describe their content. As a result, there is no need to directly observe behavior or to ask a set of respondents to reply to scales. Rather, the content analyst usually studies the content of books, magazines, newspapers, films, radio broadcasts, photographs, cartoons, letters and diaries, verbal dyadic interaction, political propaganda, or music.

Consider these examples of content analysis:

1) Investigators analyzed the major value-themes of articles published in representative "underground" periodicals (for example, *East Village Other* or *Los Angeles Free Press*) and in a set of middle-class articles (for example, from *Reader's Digest*). They found that the underground sample was significantly more "expressive"—concerned with self-expression, religion and philosophy, and human affiliation—whereas the middle-class articles were more "instrumental"—concerned with achievement, cognitive affairs, and economic interests. Based on these results, a discussion of the future of the youth underground ensued (Levin and Spates, 1970).

2) In a study of concern with wealth in the platforms of the two major parties for presidential elections from 1844 to 1964, it was found that concern with wealth has been increasing over time. Furthermore, the rate of this increase is greater for Democratic platforms than for those of the Republicans (Namenwirth, 1969).

---

* In its more restricted meaning, content analysis has long been used to categorize responses to open-ended questions in interviews or questionnaires. For this reason, the survey researcher must have an understanding of content analytic techniques.

3) An analysis of popular song lyrics in 1955 and 1966 revealed increasingly greater value placed on autonomy in boy-girl relationships over this eleven year period. The new pattern included (1) the reduction of love to physical attraction, (2) lack of permanence of the boy-girl relationship, and (3) greater activism in determining the character of the relationship (Carey, 1969).

At an abstract level, many of the procedures for conducting a content analysis differ very little from those involved in carrying out survey research. Specifically, a content anlaysis requires the development of appropriate data collection instruments and a method for drawing a representative sample.

Sampling Content

With reference to sampling, the content analyst may sample from titles and issues of magazines, newspapers, speeches, radio broadcasts, television programs or commercials, or the like. His method of sampling—whether random, accidental, quota, or judgment—typically involves more than one level. For example, in order to draw a sample of articles from middle-class magazines published during any given one-year period, a researcher might sample (1) titles (for example, Reader's Digest or LIFE), (2) issues (Dec, April, June, and September), (3) and articles (every nth article appearing in each of the selected issues).

The Recording Sheet

In regard to data collection instruments, content analysis has its peculiar set of problems and procedures. To begin with, it is not necessary to construct a questionnaire or interview schedule, since a set of respondents is not involved. Instead, the content analyst must develop a *recording sheet* with which data from his sample of content can be taken.

Problems associated with the recording sheet are of three kinds: (1) those concerned with the selection of a coding unit, (2) those relating to the development of categories, and (3) those concerned with coding.

(1) The Coding Unit

In order to conduct a content analysis, the reseacher must select a *coding unit*—the exact unit of content that he seeks to measure. Depending upon the exact nature of the study, a coding unit can vary from a single-word, phrase, paragraph or character to an entire article, story, film, or broadcast.

The nature of the recording sheet depends in part upon the choice of a coding unit. If, for example, the coding unit turns out to be a fictional character portrayed in popular short stories, then the investigator must prepare a recording sheet on each and every such character that he encounters in his sample. If the coding unit is an entire film, then he must produce a recording sheet for every film sampled.

(2) Categories

Once the coding unit has been selected, the content analyst must come up with a measurement strategy. Content analysis relies very much in this regard upon the construction of *categories* into which content can be placed. The basic requirement is that *every case—whether a fictional character, word, article, film, or the like—must be placed in one and only one category.* This indicates that the categories must be nonoverlapping or *mutually exclusive.* Thus, a fictional character classified as "male" cannot also be classified as "female"; any article labeled "expressive" cannot also be labeled "instrumental." The requirement also signifies that the categories must be *exhaustive* : there must be a place for every case that comes up. To illustrate, imagine a content analysis in which all fictional characters are to be classified as either "male" or "female." Where would we categorize an animal that is assigned a leading role or a human character whose sex is not revealed by an author? In the former case, it may be necessary to expand the original category system to include "animals." Or either case might be handled by including a miscellaneous category in which such exceptions can be placed.

A portion of a recording sheet containing the categories employed in a study of the characters in magazine short stories is located on page 54.

(3) Coding

Coding entails the procedure whereby the data are collected and the sample of content is actually categorized. For this purpose, it is not unusual to have only one or two individuals code the entire sample of content.

Under such conditions, how do we know that the findings of a content analysis reflect more than the judgment of a single coder? How does a content analysis differ from the more subjective analysis that any of us can conduct without formal training or preparation?

In order to assure the objectivity of a content analysis—especially of an analysis carried out by a single coder—the researcher must carefully define

RECORDING SHEET

Title of Story_____ Story #_____

Character's Name_____

Description of the Character_____

_____

_____

_____

1— National Residence:

    1— American
    2—Foreign
    3—Uncertain

2—Specific Nationality:

_____

3—Race:

    1—White
    2—Black
    3—Other (specify)_____
    4—Uncertain

4—Religion:

    1—Protestant
    2—Catholic
    3—Jewish
    4—Other (specify) _____
    5—Uncertain

5— Role:

    1— Star Hero (Heroine)
    2—Star Villain
    3—Other Star
    4—Supporting Player
    5—Bit Player

6—Sex:

    1—Male
    2—Female
    3—Uncertain

7—Age:

    1—Child
    2—Teenager
    3—Young Adult
    4—Middle Aged
    5—Old Age
    6—Age changes, flashback
    7—Uncertain

all categories and instruct his coder in the use of the recording sheet. As a result, a written set of instructions and precise definitions must be constructed to accompany the recording sheet. In order to determine certain characteristics of fictional characters, for example, a researcher might instruct his coders as follows (See the recording sheet above):

Coding Instructions

This is an attempt to determine what images of ethnic group members are depicted in popular magazine fiction. For each character in a story—no matter how important or unimportant his role—we hope to measure a number of characteristics including nationality, race, religion, role, sex, and age.

Not all characters will be specifically identified on all of the above characteristics. Thus certain "indicators" should be noted. It is important that you do not take wild or unwarranted guesses. Do not "presume" too much. Presumption should not be eliminated altogether, however. On the contrary, a limited degree is desirable, particularly where the social characteristics of the characters are not explicit. In such cases, there may be implicit indicators that the character belongs in one category or another. Sometimes there is too little information (e.g. minor characters, bit players, etc.) to presume anything.

In short, you should aim for a relatively high degree of certainty so that your decision will be consistent with that of other coders of the same material. High inter-coder agreement can be expected only if you read each story carefully, familiarize yourself with instructions and coding sheets, pay close attention to the description of characters, and have reasonable bases for decisions when writing information on recording sheets. Remember that too much information is better than too little. Try to be complete and be sure to positively mark each item according to the directions below.

Character's Name. Specify the name of the character where possible. If unspecified use a descriptive term (e.g. "nurse #1," etc.).

Description. Briefly define the character's dramatic role (i.e. what were some of his noteworthy characteristics, what did he do, with whom did he interact, etc.).

Item #1 (National Residence). Did the character live in the United States or in a foreign country? Circle the appropriate number. Here presumption may play a major role in your judgment and subtle indicators may be applied. Such implicit indicators include but are not limited to (1) name of character (American: Eleanor Madison, Doris Baldwin, Bill Davis, Dick Ferris, etc.), (2) language (3) general appearance, and (4) setting. You may find that a combination of implicit indicators provides a reasonable basis for certainty. Much better, of course, is the explicit indication of national residence (Robert Thompson was a *Texan*, but his visit to Paris ...).

Probably the most frequently employed indicator of national residence is setting. If it is clear that the story takes place in the United States, and no mention is made of foreign visitors, the coder may assume—when all other indicators appear consistent with the judgment—that the characters are American.

Item #2 (Specific Nationality). Where you have determined the character's national residence in Item #1 as "foreign" the next step is to ascertain his specific nationality (e.g. Italian, French, English, German, Japanese, Chinese, etc.) Where the character is American, you would place him in terms of national origin (e.g. Italian-American, English-American, French-American German-American, Japanese-American, etc.). Write this information in the space provided. If you are uncertain write "uncertain" or "unidentifiable" in the space provided for your response.

Item #3 (Race). Where you determine the character's racial identity as either white or black, circle the appropriate number. Where the character is of some other race (e.g. oriental) circle "3" and specify that group in the space provided. If you are uncertain, write in "4,"

Item #4 (Religion). The major American religious groups are represented in Item #4. Again, circle the number of whichever is applicable. Where you are uncertain, write in "5"; where an unrepresented religious group is determined specify in the space provided.

Indicators for Items 1 through 4 . It is rare to find explicit identification of characters on all measures of ethnic identification (nationality, race, and religion). Explicit identification, as in the following examples, enables the coder to come to a reliable decision. Examples: "John was a dark *Negro*"; "John was an *Italian-American*"; "John was *Catholic*."

Very often, the coder must rely for information upon *implicit* indicators of nationality, race, and religion. The following indicators have been useful in the past:

1) Appearance of Character. This may be particularly valuable in determining racial identity (references to color of skin, eyes, hair). Photographs, pictures, and written description may be used in combination.

2) Name of Character. For example, "Sven Borsen" or "Marty Spinelli" suggest the nationalities of Scandinavian and Italian. Used in conjunction with other indicators, name of character may be useful.

3) Setting. The setting is a particularly useful indicator of national residence.

4) Language. This indicator may be used with others to establish nationality or national origin.

5) Ethnic Symbols. In attempting to determine religious identity, for example, the coder might find reference to a synagogue, ethnic foods, or other objects peculiar to certain ethnic groups. Again, it is necessary to use this indicator in conjunction with others for positive identification.

Item #5 (Role). Circle the appropriate number representing one of the following dramatic roles:

1-Star Hero: highly significant to the plot and a "good guy" with positive valence.

2-Star Villain: highly significant to the plot and a "bad guy" with negative valence.

3-Other Star Player: highly significant to the plot and "neutral"— neither a good guy nor a bad guy.

4-Supporting Player: moderately significant to the plot.

5-Bit Player: relatively inconsequential to the plot.

Item #6 (Sex). Circle the appropriate number. If you are uncertain circle "3."

Item #7 (Age). Circle the appropriate number from the following list:

1-Child: an infant through age 12.

2-Teen-Ager: ages 13 through 19.

3-Young Adult: 20 through the middle thirties.

4-Middle Age: past the middle thirties through middle fifties.

5-Old Age: past the middle fifties.

If the age of the character changes from one period to another, as when the narrator tells of his childhood, or a flashback, circle "6." Where uncertain, circle "7."

The adequacy of categories, their definitions, and instructions for their use, can be determined by subjecting a small amount of content ("a sample of the sample") to a test of intercoder reliability. To the extent that a coder objectively categorizes the content according to the definitions and instructions he has been given, his coding decisions should agree with the coding decisions of other trained coders who employ identical recording sheets, instructions, and definitions. If, for example, we learn that three coders independently decide that a particular character is a "star hero," we can be relatively sure that this is a reliable judgment—a judgment made independently of the biases or preconceptions of any particular coder. As a result, it usually makes sense to carry out a test of intercoder reliability before the data are actually collected. This can be done by having several individuals code a small sample of content (say, five or ten percent of the content under study) and comparing their judgments. If this procedure yields a satisfactory level of agreement, the content analysis can proceed. If, however, the judgments of the coders tend to disagree, then the researcher might consider better defining his categories, expanding or reducing the number of categories, or modifying his instructions.

Secondary Analysis

At a growing number of colleges and universities, data generated by professional research groups are being stored on IBM cards or magnetic tapes and are available to the student. Once he learns the simple tasks of reading a codebook and accessing tape or card data, the student can conduct a secondary analysis of sets of professionally collected and processed data. By *secondary analysis*, we mean that the student tests his hypotheses on data that were originally collected and analyzed by others for some other purpose.

A secondary analysis frees the student from the tasks of collecting and processing data, so that he can concentrate more on the development and analysis of his problem. Moreover, many professional research groups employ well-designed and executed sampling plans and have data collected by carefully trained interviewers.

The major problem associated with secondary analysis has to do with securing data that properly "fit" the student's problem-area or hypotheses. Interesting data concerning characteristics of student radicals may be worthless to a student who seeks to test a hypothesis about attitudes in a public housing project. On the other hand, a perusal of the survey questions contained in project codebooks often stimulates new ideas for conducting research, especially if the student is not closed with respect to possible topics.

A final word about secondary analysis: it frequently gives the student an opportunity to work with *aggregate data*, data in which the unit of analysis is a *group* of individuals (such as a city, state or nation) rather than the individual per se. Aggregate data can be secured from relatively reliable sources such as the Bureau of the Census or UNESCO. Moreover, it can be transposed with relative ease from tables and charts to IBM cards or magnetic tapes. Finally, since most aggregate data are based upon an entire population and not merely a sample, the student who employs aggregate data may have the opportunity to directly study a population.

Aggregate data can sometimes provide a satisfactory alternative to surveys in which the individual serves as the unit of analysis. For instance, a student might test the relationship between level of income and party identification by recording for each state "per-capita income" and "proportion of the vote for Democratic candidates." Similarly, the relationship between frustration and prejudice might be examined among Southern states by relating annual changes in the price of cotton to the rate at which blacks were lynched.

Collecting the Data: A Comparison of Methods

In the present chapter, we have been introduced to experiments, surveys, content analysis, and secondary analysis—widely differing approaches to the collection of data, each having its characteristic weaknesses and strengths.

Experimental research is capable of establishing an association between an independent variable and a dependent variable, fixing their time-order, and ruling out spuriousness. So powerful is the experiment in this respect that it is generally regarded as the ideal model for the conduct of scientific research. By no other method does the researcher gain so great a degree of control over the collection of his data.

Despite its tremendous power to establish relationships, however, the experiment has been "underused" by certain social scientists. This has to do in part with the difficult ethical problems raised by the manipulation of human subjects. Playing an important part in this regard are issues such as the role of experimental deception per se (for example, the use of bogus aptitude examinations to vary level of frustration) as well as the psychological harm that may befall the subject of an experiment (for example, the effect on a subject's self-esteem of informing him that he has flunked a frustrating examination).

Ethical concerns represent only a part of the problem. Another important reason why experiments may be rejected can be found in the nature of social scientific variables. Many factors of interest to the social scientist do not readily lend themselves to experimental manipulation. For instance, how would we manipulate sex, race, or family structure—to mention only the most obvious? As a related matter, it is unfortunately true that those independent variables most amenable to experimental manipulation sometimes—but only sometimes—turn out to be the most trivial in nature.

A final reason often cited for lack of interest in experimental research has to do with the apparent artificiality of the typical experimental setting. Detractors argue that the experimental laboratory shares little in common with variables that operate in the "real world." Moreover, many, if not most, experiments employ accidental samples—typically a classroom of college freshmen—chosen strictly on the basis of convenience. As a result, it is difficult to make accurate generalizations even to highly restricted populations.

With reference to increasing the "real world" quality of experiments, a growing number of social scientists are coming to recognize the utility of conducting "natural" experiments—experiments that are conducted in natural settings rather than in the "artificial" confines of a laboratory. For example, a researcher might conduct a "before-after" experiment to test the effect on neighborliness of forcing families to relocate their homes in order to make way for highway construction. In addition, many social scientists have come to the conclusion that even the laboratory is "real," and that it may be important to establish causal relationships, regardless of the extent to which they can immediately be generalized.

Not unlike the experiment, survey research can be used to establish an association between independent and dependent variables. However, the survey is generally not so powerful as the experiment with respect to establishing time-order or ruling out spuriousness.

Nevertheless, survey research is easily the most popular method for testing social scientific hypotheses, especially among sociologists and political scientists. Why this should be the case is indeed not difficult to understand. In the first place, survey researchers have devised statistical methods which come to grips with many problems of time-order and spuriousness. Furthermore, the survey—in conjunction with a properly designed and executed sampling plan—can be an extremely effective way to draw generalizations from a sample to a large population. Finally, unlike experimental research in which only a few "key" variables are examined, the survey is capable of simultaneously handling numerous independent and dependent variables, so that the complex nature of social reality can be better approximated.

To an increasing extent, social scientists are coming to recognize that ethical problems are not uniquely associated with an experimental approach. On the contrary, a survey questionnaire or interview generally includes a type of deception, if only in the use of indirect and subtle questions whose true intent is kept from the respondent. Moreover, publishing the results of survey research may have serious consequences for the respondents being examined, as well as for the society as a whole. Consider the furor that would surely arise if social scientists were to study the social structure of an American community, revealing information about its "concealed" decision-makers or identifying its powerful inhabitants.*

As we have seen the respondent's awareness that he is being measured may actually affect the nature of his responses to survey or experimental instruments such as interviews or questionnaires. By contrast, content analysis avoids such problems, since it does not ask a set of respondents to reply to scales, but asks questions of the communication messages that previously have been produced.

This advantage of content analysis must be weighed against its characteristic weaknesses of reliability and sampling—weaknesses not shared by the more traditional survey and experimental methods. For example, it is sometimes difficult to determine whether a particular message of mass communication reflects the characteristics of its source, its intended audience, or the larger society in which it was created. This criticism of content analysis has been raised several times since 1940.†

The major advantage associated with secondary analysis is that of freeing the student to become more involved with his theoretical approach and the analysis of his problem. In addition, secondary analysis generally produces better quality data than can be secured from a student project conducted during a one-semester course. On the other hand, the student who chooses to conduct a secondary analysis cannot always find a "fit" between his hypotheses and the data. Moreover, such a student misses the experience— albeit often tedious and time-consuming—associated with the first-hand collection and processing of his data.

What's Ahead

In the present chapter, we have examined experiments, surveys, content analysis, and secondary analysis—widely differing approaches to the collection of data. After gathering the raw data, the researcher must analyze his results for their bearing on his initial hypotheses. The purpose of the next chapter is to provide the tools for such an analysis.

Exercises

1) Taking a single social scientific hypothesis of your (or your instructor's) choice, briefly explain how you might go about testing this hypothesis by

---

* For a discussion of the reactions to just such a research outcome, see Becker (1964).

† See, for example, the comments in Gans (1972).

means of (a) an experiment, (b) a survey, (c) a content analysis, and (d) a secondary analysis.

2) For a hypothesis taken from the literature or originated by you, develop appropriate before-after *and* after-only experimental designs to test the effect of an independent variable on a dependent variable. Illustrate graphically both of your experimental designs.

3) For the hypothesis in Exercise #2 above, add a category to the independent variable and modify your experimental designs accordingly. Illustrate graphically.

4) For the hypothesis in Exercise #2 above, add an independent variable and modify your experimental designs accordingly. Illustrate graphically.

5) Construct a self-administered questionnaire *and* an interview schedule to collect the following data from a large sample of college students:

   a) Sex of respondent
   b) Age of respondent
   c) Income of respondent's father
   d) Political party affiliation of respondent
   e) Respondent's participation in voluntary associations
   f) Neighborliness of respondent

6) Construct a recording sheet and coding instructions to be used for a content analysis of advertising models (i.e., human figures in drawings or photographs) that appear in popular magazine advertisements. Include the following information on your recording sheet for each model:

   a) Sex
   b) Age
   c) Occupation
   d) Race
   e) Degree of glamour or beauty

Try your recording sheet and instructions by coding the models appearing in any 10 magazine advertisements.

CHAPTER 5:   THE TOOLS OF ANALYSIS

In the analysis stage of a study, the data are tabulated, counted, summarized, compared, in a word, *organized*, so that the accuracy of the researcher's hypotheses can be tested. The analysis might be conducted manually or by computer.[*]

Data can be organized in many ways, depending in part upon what the researcher must know in order to evaluate his hypotheses. It is convenient to discuss the techniques that permit organizing the data—the tools of analysis—as applied to (1) the description or estimate of a single variable, and (2) the relationship between two or more variables.

The Analysis of a Single Variable

In most fact-finding research, an investigator attempts to learn something about one variable at a time. It might be his objective, for example, to describe the attitudes of a sample of respondents on a particular social or political issue, in which case he might *count* the *frequency* with which various responses occur, casting these results in the form of a *frequency distribution*. For most purposes, a frequency distribution consists of at least two columns, a left-hand column that indicates the categories of the characteristic being examined, and an adjacent column containing the frequency of occurence in each category (f). Many frequency distributions also contain a right-hand column in which the percentages for each category have been shown. This arrangement has been illustrated in Table 5-1 for the attitude distribution of a sample to the question, "Do you think that the President is doing a good job?"

---

[*] To aid the student who seeks to conduct a computer analysis of data, appendices A, B, and C at the back of the book contain information related to card punching and the use of a software program.

TABLE 5-1
A FREQUENCY DISTRIBUTION OF ATTITUDES

Responses to the question, "Do you think that the president is doing a good job?"	f	%
1—Very Good Job	10	17
2—Good Job	20	33
3—Not Sure	15	25
4—Bad Job	10	17
5—Very Bad Job	5	8
	N = 60	100%

Measures of Central Tendency

The research objective is often served by constructing a *summary description* of the frequency distribution. Such a measure describes the data by its "average" or "typical" value and is referred to as a *measure of central tendency*. The three best-known measures of central tendency—the mode, median, and mean—will be discussed here.

The *mode* (Mo.) is the category or score value that occurs most often in a distribution. In Table 5-1, for example, category #2, "Good Job," represents the mode, since it was the most frequently selected by this sample of respondents.

By contrast, the *median* (Mdn) is the middlemost point in a distribution, that measure of central tendency which cuts the distribution into 2 equal parts when the scores have been arranged in order of size. In Table 5-1, the median is approximately 2.5; half of the 60 responses fall above and half fall below this value.

The most popular measure of central tendency, the *mean* ($\overline{X}$) or arithmetic average, is defined as the sum of a set of scores divided by the total number of scores. The mean can be computed by the formula

$$\overline{X} = \frac{\Sigma X}{N}$$

where:

$\overline{X}$ = the mean (read as "X bar")
Σ = the sum of the scores
X = a raw score in the distribution
N = the total number of scores

When a large number of individual scores are collected for which the mean must be obtained, the total frequency of each category or score value may be multiplied by its score value, summed, and divided by the number of responses. This procedure yields a mean score as follows:

Response	Score Value	f	X
Very Good Job	1	10	10
Good Job	2	20	40
Not Sure	3	15	45
Bad Job	4	10	40
Very Bad Job	5	5	25
		N = 60	$\Sigma X = 160$

Therefore,

$$\overline{X} = \frac{160}{60}$$
$$= 2.67$$

A mean score of 2.67 indicates that the "average" response in Table 5-1 falls between "good job" and "not sure," though slightly closer to the latter.

How do we choose among the three measures of central tendency—the mode, median, and mean? The mode is properly regarded as a preliminary or rough indicator of central tendency—one that can be obtained by simple inspection. To the extent that a precise measure of central tendency is desired, the choice is generally between the median and the mean. The median is more stable than the mean—less affected by extreme score values—when applied to highly skewed or assymetrical distributions, distributions in which there are extreme scores in only one direction, either high or low. It is also true, however, that the mean can be better used for advanced statistical analyses. As a result, the mean is usually selected over the median for the purpose of describing distributions in which extreme skewness does not exist.

Measures of Dispersion

Used by itself, any measure of central tendency yields only an incomplete picture of a set of data. In addition to a measure of central tendency, we need an index of how the scores are scattered or dispersed around the "average" or "typical" value in the distribution. We need a measure of

TABLE 5-2

HYPOTHETICAL DISTRIBUTIONS OF PER CAPITA INCOME

Distribution A		Distribution B	
X	x	X	x
$5000	−2714	$7000	−755
3000	−4714	8428	+673
10000	+2286	7000	−755
6000	−1714	8428	+673
6000	−1714	8428	+673
9000	+1286	7000	−755
15000	+7286	8000	+245
$\Sigma X = \$54000$	$\Sigma|x| = 21714$	$\Sigma X = \$54284$	$\Sigma|x| = 4529$

$$\overline{X} = \frac{54000}{7} = \$7714 \qquad\qquad \overline{X} = \frac{54284}{7} = \$7755$$

$$R = \$12001 \qquad\qquad\qquad R = \$429$$

$$AD = \frac{21714}{7} = \$3102 \qquad\qquad AD = \frac{4529}{7} = \$647$$

dispersion. Three measures are frequently employed for this purpose: the range, average deviation, and standard deviation.

The *range* (R) of a set of scores is the distance between the lowest and highest scores plus one; "one" being added to the result in order to include both end points. To find the range, therefore, the lowest score is subtracted from the highest score and one is added to this result. In Table 5-2, the range of scores in Distribution A is $12001 whereas the range of scores in Distribution B is only $1429. Thus, Distribution A has greater dispersion of scores than does Distribution B.

Unlike the range, the *average deviation* (AD) takes into account every score value in a distribution, a characteristic giving it great precision. More specifically, the average deviation indicates how much, on the average, the scores deviate or depart from the mean of a distribution. Expressed symbolically,

$$AD = \frac{\Sigma |x|}{N}$$

where:

AD = the average deviation

x = a deviation score*

---

* $x = X - \overline{X}$. For example, if the mean is 20 and a raw score is 25, then $x = 25 - 20 = +5$, indicating that this raw score falls 5 raw score units above the mean.

$\sum |X|$ = the sum of the absolute deviations (disregarding plus and minus signs)

N = the total number of scores

Referring back to Table 5-2, we see that for Distribution A, AD = \$3102, while for Distribution B, AD = \$647. Clearly, then, the scores in Distribution A are dispersed more widely than are the scores in Distribution B.

Let us summarize the step-by-step procedure for computing the average deviation:

1) Find the mean for the distribution;

2) Subtract the mean from each raw score and add these deviations, ignoring their signs;

3) Divide by N.

Before leaving the topic of dispersion, we must examine the nature of an especially useful, though complex, measure. Known as the *standard deviation* (SD), this measure of dispersion can be technically defined as the square root of the mean of the squared deviations from the mean of a distribution. Thus, not unlike the average deviation, SD indicates how raw scores deviate, on the average, from their mean. Also like the average deviation, the standard deviation is based upon the procedure of finding and combining deviation scores—scores representing the distance of raw scores from their mean.

It is fortunately true that the standard deviation has an important advantage not shared by the average deviation. Whereas the average deviation ignores plus and minus signs and uses absolute deviation scores, the standard deviation instead employs the mathematically acceptable procedure of clearing the signs by squaring deviations. As a result, the standard deviation is often employed as the initial step in conducting more advanced statistical analyses.

By formula,

$$SD = \sqrt{\frac{\sum x^2}{N}}$$

where:

SD = the standard deviation

$\sum x^2$ = the sum of the squared deviations from the mean

N = the total number of scores

For Distribution A in Table 5-2, the standard deviation can be found as follows:

X	x	x^2
$5000	−2714	7365796
3000	−4714	22221796
10000	+2286	5225796
6000	−1714	2937796
6000	−1714	2937796
9000	+1286	1653796
15000	+7286	53085796
$\Sigma X = \$54000$		$\Sigma x^2 = 95428572$

$$SD = \sqrt{\frac{95428572}{7}}$$

$$= \sqrt{13632653}$$

$$= 3692$$

Thus, the standard deviation of the scores in Distribution A is 3692. Let us summarize the procedure for computing the standard deviation:
1) Find the mean for the distribution;
2) Subtract the mean from each raw score to get deviation;
3) Square each deviation before adding the squared deviations together;
4) Divide by N and get the square root of this result.

As in the case of the range and the average deviation, the larger the size of the standard deviation, the greater the dispersion of scores around their mean. Further interpretation of the standard deviation very much depends upon having an understanding of a particular kind of frequency distribution, one commonly known as the bell shaped or *normal distribution*. Approximately six standard deviations cover almost 100% of the cases in a normal distribution—three SDs fall above and three SDs fall below the mean. It is also true that roughly 34% of the cases in a normal distribution lie between its mean and the raw score which falls one standard deviation in either direction from the mean, regardless of the nature of the characteristic being measured. Thus, if the mean of a normal distribution of examination grades is 70 with a standard deviation of 5, we know that approximately 34% of these students got grades between 70 and 75 and another 34% between 65 and 70 since X = 75 and X = 65 lie exactly one standard deviation above and below the mean respectively (70 + 5 = 75; 70 − 5 = 65). Further understanding of the nature of the normal distribution requires detailed discussion not possible in this brief presentation.*

Statistical Assumptions

Statistical measures make assumptions about the data to which they can be applied. For instance, most of the measures we have thus far encountered—the mean, range, average deviation, and standard deviation—require the use of interval data. Because the median divides a sequence of values into two equal parts, these values must be susceptible only to ranking. For this reason, the median can be applied to ordinal or interval data. By contrast, the mode can be applied at any level of measurement, requiring only the categorization of data.

The Analysis of a Relationship

As we have seen, fact-finding research focuses on one variable at a time. Clearly this is not true of explanatory research, since it seeks to describe the nature of a relationship between two or more variables. In conducting explanatory research, a student has at least two alternatives, depending upon the level at which his data have been measured and upon his skills with respect to data analysis: 1) to arrange the data in a contingency table, drawing conclusions from appropriate cell frequencies and column subtotals, or 2) to correlate his variables and interpret the meaning of the resultant correlation coefficient.

Contingency Table Analysis

A *contingency table* presents all possible combinations of the score values or categories that result when two or more variables have been related. For instance, in order to test the hypothesis that college-aged youth tend to identify with the political orientation of their fathers, we might conduct a survey in which the following question is addressed separately to both father and child:

Which political party do you generally identify with?

1_____Democrat
2_____Republican
3_____Independent

---

* For more detailed discussion of the characteristics of the normal curve, see Levin (1973).

In the present example, the political orientation of the child can be treated as a dependent variable capable of being explained in part by the political orientation of the father, the independent variable.

Contingency Table 5-3 below presents hypothetical results obtained for the relationship between the independent variable, father's political orientation (located in the columns), and the dependent variable, child's political orientation (located in the rows). These data have been shown as *cell frequencies*; that is, the number in each cell represents the number of father-child combinations that selected the answer represented by that particular cell. For example, the upper, left-hand cell (f = 80) indicates that 80 youths whose fathers identify with the Democratic party similarly consider themselves to be Democrats.

Notice also that percentages for each cell have been given in parentheses. In accordance with the conventional arrangement, these percentages are shown by the categories of the independent variable and therefore are totalled by column. From these percentages, we see,

1. of all fathers who identify with the Democratic Party, 73% of their children also identify with that party,

2. of all fathers who identify with the Republican party, 74% of their children also identify with that party,

3. of all fathers who identify themselves as independents, 100% of their children also identify themselves as independents.

Thus, in every column of Table 5-3, a substantial majority of these youth identify with the political orientation of their fathers. On this basis, the researcher might reasonably conclude that the data tend to confirm his initial hypothesis.

Contingency table analysis can be expanded to include any number of variables, limited only by the ability of the researcher to find enough respondents and to organize his data in a theoretically meaningful way. In

TABLE 5-3

THE RELATIONSHIP BETWEEN FATHER'S POLITICAL ORIENTATION
AND CHILD'S POLITICAL ORIENTATION: HYPOTHETICAL DATA

Child's Political Orientation:		Father's Political Orientation		
		Democratic	Republican	Independent
		f	f	f
Democratic		80 (73%)	10 (13%)	–
Republican		20 (18%)	60 (74%)	–
Independent		10 (9%)	10 (13%)	110 (100%)
	N =	110 (100%)	80 (100%)	110 (100%)

TABLE 5-4

THE RELATIONSHIP BETWEEN POLITICAL ORIENTATION OF FATHER
AND CHILD BY SEX OF THE CHILD: HYPOTHETICAL DATA

Child's Political Orientation	Males			Females		
	Father's Political Orientation:					
	Demo-cratic	*Repub-lican*	*Inde-pendent*	*Demo-cratic*	*Repub-lican*	*Inde-pendent*
	f	f	f	f	f	f
Democratic	50 (78%)	4 (9%)	–	30 (65%)	6 (17%)	–
Republican	10 (16%)	36 (80%)	–	10 (22%)	24 (69%)	–
Independent	4 (6%)	5 (11%)	45(100%)	6 (13%)	5 (14%)	65(100%)
N =	64(100%)	45(100%)	45(100%)	46(100%)	35(100%)	65(100%)

this regard, it is often desirable to construct three-dimensional contingency tables in which the relationship between an independent variable and a dependent variable can be examined in the light of a third variable. The many uses of such three-dimensional contingency tables include (1) testing the spuriousness of a relationship when a third factor is suspected of explaining it, and (2) testing the limits to which a relationship can be generalized.

Returning to the example in Table 5-3, we might begin to test the limits of this relationship by constructing a three-dimensional contingency table in which the relationship between the political orientation of father and child is examined separately by the sex of the child. As shown in Table 5-4, we can determine from this three-dimensional contingency table that boys were more likely than girls to follow the political convictions of their fathers, when their fathers identified themselves as either Republicans or Democrats. For instance, among fathers with a Democratic party identity, 78% of the boys but only 65% of the girls similarly identified themselves as Democrats. We find, therefore, that the relationship between the political orientation of father and child may tend to hold better for boys than it does for girls.

Until this point in our discussion of contingency tables, we have implicitly assumed that the researcher will actually study the entire population in which he has an interest. As we have seen in Chapter 4, however, this is generally not the case, for the researcher typically investigates only a sample drawn from a given population of individuals or groups. In the foregoing illustration, for instance, the 300 father-child combinations interviewed might easily have been taken at random from a much larger group of fathers and their children. As we already know, the procedure of random sampling makes it possible to generalize from a sample to a specified population.

Even given the most effective random sampling procedures, however, there will *always* be some difference between a sample and its population. Arising out of the very nature of the procedure of taking a sample, this difference—known as *sampling error*—is strictly the product of chance and does not result from any mistake or carelessness on the part of a researcher.

In the face of inevitable sampling error, how is it possible to determine whether a relationship between variables as found in a sample actually reflects a relationship in the population? The answer can be found in the nature of a *test of significance*, a method to determine the probability that a relationship found in a sample might be a product of chance or sampling error. The question becomes: if the research were repeated one hundred times (that is, in one hundred random samples drawn from the same population), how many times would this relationship occur by chance—*given no relationship in the population?*

There are numerous tests of significance, each having its peculiar set of assumptions for appropriate usage. We shall discuss only that test of significance commonly known as *chi square* (X^2), since it is applicable to nominal data, the kind illustrated in Table 5-3.

The chi square test of significance is based upon comparing the cell frequencies of a contingency table that can be *expected* on the basis of chance if there is no relationship (f_e) and the cell frequencies actually *observed* in a random sample of respondents (f_o). The greater the difference between (f_e) and (f_o), the more likely it is that the relationship found in a sample is representative of a relationship in the population.

Observed frequencies are the cell frequencies actually obtained when a study is conducted and data are collected. Thus, the data in Table 5-3 are observed frequencies. Expected frequencies can be obtained for any cell by multiplying its row and column marginals and dividing by the total N. In Table 5-3, for example, f_e for the upper left-hand cell (democratic-democratic) is

$$\frac{(90)(110)}{300} = 33.$$

Similarly, f_e for the lower left-hand cell (democratic-independent) is

$$\frac{(130)(110)}{300} = 47.67$$

All observed and expected frequencies for the cells in Table 5-3 have been shown in Table 5-5 below:

TABLE 5-5
OBSERVED AND EXPECTED FREQUENCIES FOR TABLE 5-3

Child's Political Orientation:	Father's Political Orientation						ROW MARGINALS
	Democratic		Republican		Independent		
	f_o	f_e	f_o	f_e	f_o	f_e	
Democratic	80	33	10	24	–	33	90
Republican	20	29.33	60	21.33	–	29.33	80
Independent	10	47.67	10	34.67	110	47.67	130
COLUMN MARGINALS	110		80		110		N = 300

Once both expected and observed cell frequencies have been assigned, chi square can be obtained by the formula,

$$X^2 = \sum \frac{(f_o - f_e)^2}{f_e}$$

In the present example,

$$X^2 = \frac{(80 - 33)^2}{33} + \frac{(20 - 29.33)^2}{29.33} + \frac{(10 - 47.67)^2}{47.67} + \frac{(10 - 24)^2}{24}$$
$$+ \frac{(60 - 21.33)^2}{21.33} + \frac{(10 - 34.67)^2}{34.67} + \frac{(0 - 33)^2}{33} + \frac{(0 - 29.33)^2}{29.33}$$
$$+ \frac{(110 - 47.67)^2}{47.67}$$
$$= 339.34$$

In the social sciences, if a sample relationship could occur by chance (or sampling error) five times or less in one hundred (P=.05), it is generally regarded as being *statistically significant* or representative of a relationship in the population. The larger an obtained X^2 value, the less likely it is that the relationship could occur by chance alone.

In the present example, our obtained $X^2 = 339.34$. To determine how often this value could occur by chance, we need (1) a table of critical values of X^2 such as that found in the appendix of most elementary statistics texts, and (2) the number of *degrees of freedom* for our particular problem.

The degrees of freedom (df) for any X^2 problem can be obtained by the formula,

$$df = (C - 1)(R - 1)$$

where:

    df = degrees of freedom
    C = number of columns in contingency table
    R = number of rows in contingency table

Thus, for the problem at hand,

$$df = (3 - 1)(3 - 1)$$

$$= 4$$

Having obtained a X^2 value and the degrees of freedom for the problem, we can proceed to a table of critical values of X^2—values of chi square that could occur by chance only 5 times in 100 samples. Selected critical values of $X^2(P = .05)$ have been reproduced below:

df	$X^2(P = .05)$
1	3.84
2	5.99
3	7.82
4	9.49
5	11.07

We have already determined that df = 4 for the chi square problem in Table 5-5. As a result, the appropriate critical value of $X^2 = 9.49$. Specifically, in order to conclude that a statistically significant result has been obtained—a result that is indeed representative of a relationship in the population and not just sampling error—our *obtained* value of X^2 must *equal* or *exceed* the critical value of $X^2(P = .05)$ as located in the table. Since our obtained $X^2 = 339.34$ —a much larger value than the table value—it is possible to conclude that our result probably reflects a relationship in the population. In other words, a chi square value of 339.34 could occur by chance, *but* only less than 5 times in 100! It seems reasonable to conclude, therefore, that this population of youth actually do tend to identify with the political orientations of their fathers.

Correlation Analysis

Correlation analysis is, in one sense, simpler and, in another, more difficult than an analysis conducted by means of a contingency table.

Correlation is simpler because the researcher is confronted with a single statistic—a correlation coefficient—rather than with a matrix of cell frequencies and their column totals. It is more difficult because the researcher must learn how properly to interpret the correlation coefficient that he obtains, sometimes without making direct reference to the original distribution of scores.

A *correlation coefficient* is a measure of association between two variables, a measure which expresses both the strength and the direction of a relationship. With respect to the degree or strength of a correlation, most coefficients range between -1.00 and $+1.00$; the closer to 1.00 in either direction, plus or minus, the stronger the relationship between the two variables. Thus, a correlation coefficient of $+.98$ or $-.92$ indicates a very strong—nearly perfect—relationship, whereas a coefficient close to zero such as $-.10$ or $+.07$ signifies an extremely weak relationship. A "zero correlation" $(.00)$ represents no relationship between the variables.

The direction of correlation can be regarded as either positive or negative. A *positive correlation* such as that between education and income occurs when respondents getting high scores on one variable (many years of school) also tend to get high scores on the other variable (high income); conversely, respondents who obtain low scores on one variable (few years of school) tend to obtain low scores on the other (low income). By contrast, a *negative correlation* as between socio-economic status and certain types of criminality such as breaking-and-entering indicates that respondents who get high scores on the first variable (high status) tend to get low scores on the second variable (low criminality); conversely, those respondents getting low scores on the first variable (low status) get high scores on the second (high criminality). Regarding the direction of a relationship, minus numerical values of a correlation coefficient indicate the presence of a negative correlation (for instance, $-.25$, $-.83$, or $-.57$), whereas plus numerical values indicate the presence of a positive correlation (for instance, $+.25$, $+.83$, or $+.57$).

We will illustrate the procedure for obtaining *Pearson r*, a widely employed correlation coefficient for data of the interval level of measurement. Let us suppose that a researcher studies a randomly drawn sample of seven father-child combinations in an effort to test the hypothesis that children tend to adopt the political orientation of their fathers. Let us also say that this researcher constructs a measure of political conservatism which he administers to the members of his sample, both fathers and children (higher scores on the measure indicating greater conservatism).

The resultant scores of political conservatism for these fathers (X) and their children (Y) have been shown in Table 5-6. We can see from these data, for instance, that father A got a score of 8 while his child received a score of 6, indicating that this father was slightly more conservative then his child.

TABLE 5-6
SCORES OF POLITICAL CONSERVATISM FOR FATHERS
AND THEIR CHILDREN

	Father's Score(X)	*Child's Score*(Y)
A	8	6
B	10	10
C	2	4
D	5	3
E	1	2
F	5	7
G	4	6

To apply the Pearson r formula to the foregoing problem, we must obtain $\sum X, \sum Y, \sum X^2, \sum Y^2$, and $\sum XY$ as follows:

X	X²	Y	Y²	XY
8	64	6	36	48
10	100	10	100	100
2	4	4	16	8
5	25	3	9	15
1	1	2	4	2
5	25	7	49	35
4	16	6	36	24
$\sum X = 35$	$\sum X^2 = 235$	$\sum Y = 38$	$\sum Y^2 = 250$	$\sum XY = 232$

We can now apply the following Pearson r formula:

$$r = \frac{N \sum XY - (\sum X)(\sum Y)}{\sqrt{[N \sum X^2 - (\sum X)^2][N \sum Y^2 - (\sum Y)^2]}}$$

where:

r = the Pearson correlation coefficient
N = the total number of pairs of scores X and Y
X = raw score on the X variable
Y = raw score on the Y variable

Therefore,

$$r = \frac{7(232) - (35)(38)}{\sqrt{[(7)(235) - (1225)][(7)(250) - (1444)]}}$$

$$= \frac{1624 - 1330}{\sqrt{(1645 - 1225)(1750 - 1444)}}$$

$$= \frac{294}{\sqrt{128520}}$$

$$= \frac{294}{358.5}$$

$$= +.82$$

A correlation coefficient of +.82 indicates the presence of a rather strong positive relationship between the political orientation of father and child. Specifically, the more conservative the father, the more conservative his child tends to be. Notice also, however, that we have demonstrated only that a correlation exists in the small sample of seven father-child dyads being studied—not in the population of father-child dyads from which this sample was taken.

Just as in the case of a contingency table analysis, we must now determine whether our sample result represents a population characteristic or merely a sampling error. For this purpose, we must locate (1) a table of critical values of r such as that found in the appendix of most elementary statistics texts, and (2) the number of degrees of freedom for our problem.

The degrees of freedom (df) for any value of Pearson r can be obtained by the formula,

$$df = N - 2$$

where:

   df = degrees of freedom
   N = the number of pairs of scores X and Y
Thus, for the foregoing problem,

$$df = 7 - 2$$

$$= 5$$

Once r and the number of degrees of freedom have been determined, we proceed to a table of critical values of r—values that could occur by chance only 5 times in 100 samples. Selected critical values of r (P=.05) are shown below:

df	r(P = .05)
4	± .81
5	± .76
6	± .71
7	± .67
8	± .63
9	± .60
10	± .58

For the data in Table 5-6, the appropriate critical value of r equals .76. That is to say, in order to conclude that a statistically significant correlation has been obtained—a correlation that is indeed representative of a relationship in the population and not just sampling error—our *obtained* value of r must *equal* or *exceed* the critical value of r(P = .05) listed in the table. Since the obtained r = +.82 —a larger value than that required in the table—it becomes possible to conclude that a correlation between the political conservatism of father and child probably exists in the population from which the sample was drawn. To be sure, a Pearson r of ± .82 could occur by chance, *but* only less than 5 times in every 100 studies. On this basis, it is reasonable to conclude that children actually tend to adopt the political orientations of their fathers.

What's Ahead

The task of the present chapter was to identify and discuss some of the tools of analysis with which the researcher organizes the masses of raw data that he collects. Having gathered and analyzed his data, the researcher must now interpret and report the findings, applying them to his research hypotheses and discussing their implications. In Chapter 6, these final stages in the conduct of social science research are examined.

Exercises

1) Eight students were questioned regarding their attitudes toward Puerto Ricans. These responses on a scale from 1 to 10 (higher scores indicate

more favorable attitudes toward Puerto Ricans) were as follows:

Respondent	X
A	8
B	7
C	7
D	4
E	3
F	3
G	3
H	2

For the attitude scores above, find (a) the mode, (b) the median, (c) the mean, (d) the range, (e) the average deviation, and (f) the standard deviation.

2) Random samples of males and females in a particular college were interviewed to determine whether or not they belonged to the Democratic Party. It was found that 29 out of 35 males were Democrats; 14 out of 30 females were Democrats. Conducting a contingency table analysis and computing a chi square test of significance, test the hypothesis that males are more likely than females to belong to the Democratic Party. What do your results indicate?

3) The ten white Protestant students below were interviewed about (X) their attitudes toward Blacks and (Y) their attitudes toward Jews. Compute a Pearson correlation coefficient for this data in order to determine whether attitude toward Jews is associated with attitude toward Blacks. What do your results suggest?

Student	X	Y
A	10	8
B	1	4
C	4	5
D	5	5
E	4	6
F	3	1
G	9	7
H	8	10
I	8	7
J	3	4

CHAPTER 6: COMPLETING THE RESEARCH REPORT

After analyzing his data, the student's most important task in completing a research report is to present his findings in the light of his hypothesis and the theory from which it has been derived. Do the results tend to support or disprove the initial expectations of the researcher? This question cannot be ignored, but must be faced squarely and discussed thoroughly. In Chapter 5, for instance, results are presented which lend support to the hypothesis that children tend to adopt the political orientations of their fathers. Such conclusions must be carefully drawn from the analysis of results with the aid of devices such as contingency tables or correlation coefficients, and should be explicitly stated with reference to the hypotheses of the study.

Drawing Implications

Once conclusions have been derived from the data, the researcher still has before him the task of drawing relevant implications of his analysis. In most cases, this procedure involves (1) methodological implications, (2) related problem-areas, (3) ideas for future research, and (4) policy recommendations.

(1) Methodological Limitations

No study is perfectly conceived, designed, and executed. Every research project has its weaknesses as well as its strengths. Only if the reader is alerted to the limitations of a study can the conclusions of that study be viewed in their proper perspective. In a survey project, for instance, a researcher would spell out any problems he encountered in obtaining a representative sample, especially if such problems influence the extent to which his findings can be generalized. In a similar way, an experimenter might report irregularities that arise in connection with the manipulation of the treatment (for instance, suspicious comments from his subjects).

(2) Related Problem-Areas

What do the findings of a study mean vis-a-vis related problem-areas in social science? If, for example, an investigator has studied the effect of value consensus on the parent-child relationship, he might also speculate what influence consensus has on the quality of the relationship between husband and wife or between close friends. Likewise, a student who shows that people in his sample tend to vote in terms of self-interest might discuss the implications of this result for understanding the behavior of nation-states or of the family.

(3) Ideas for Future Research

Research conclusions frequently suggest ideas for conducting future research. If, for example, a student rejects or disproves a hypothesis, he might suggest a revision of the theory from which it was derived and an appropriate method for testing its implications. Or, if the hypothesis is marginally confirmed, the student might suggest a more effective way to test it.

(4) Policy Recommendations

In many projects, it is appropriate to make recommendations for policy on the basis of the confirmation or rejection of the research hypothesis. If research has determined that prejudice against black Americans diminishes when blacks and whites are assigned joint tasks in which success can only be achieved by cooperation, the investigator might discuss methods for restructuring institutions such as schools or the armed forces in order to bring about attitude change in the area of race relations. Likewise, if it is determined that certain minority groups are being discriminated against in the area of employment or education, then the researcher might suggest, for example, the advisability of introducing appropriate legislation to combat such discrimination.

Writing the Report

In accordance with the particular preferences of his field of social science and those of his instructor, the student should select a format for his research report which permits an organized reconstruction of the methods and procedures employed in conducting his research project, as well as a presentation of the major conclusions and implications of the study. This can usually be accomplished in the framework of some variation of the following suggested format: (1) background, (2) method, (3) results, and (4) discussion.

(1) Background

The first section of a research report generally contains a statement of the problem and a theoretical analysis of the problem, including hypotheses. The analysis often includes definitions of concepts, a presentation of related propositions, and any literature or observations which can be introduced in order to justify the hypotheses of the study.

The following brief excerpts from social science research illustrate some of the key elements in the presentation of a problem and its theoretical analysis:

(1) from a secondary analysis of the causes of racial disturbances, a presentation of concepts:

> In this paper we examine a number of explanations of the causes of racial disorders, then use empirical data to compare their respective abilities to account for the locations of outbreaks during the 1960's. We will follow the conceptualization of collective behavior which has been employed by other investigators and distinguish between *underlying causes* and *immediate precipitants* of racial disturbances (Spilerman, 1970, p. 628).

(2) from an experimental study in communication research, a statement of the problem:

> As the number of experimental studies on primacy-recency has grown, it has become apparent that, in the two-sided communication situation, a variety of independent variables can influence the formation and change of attitudes and opinions. Variables such as the audience's total unfamiliarity with a communication (2,3,4,16,17,18), the use of highly controversial subject matter (10), and contiguity between a rewarding event and the last-heard communication (27) have been associated with the primacy effect in opinion change. The recency effect has been associated with variables such as the audience's relative unfamiliarity with a topic (9.26) and contiguity between a punishing event and the last-heard communication (25). In addition, the influence of a considerable number of other variables for inducing primacy or recency has been investigated (6,7,8,11,13,14,19,29,30). Although some preliminary attempts have been made to embrace miscellaneous variables within the context of a single theoretical scheme (12,28), such efforts have not proved totally sucessful. One purpose of this paper is to introduce the rationale for a system that may embrace several variables (Rosnow, Holz, and Levin, 1966, p. 135).

(3) from a secondary analysis of the effects of city life on tolerance, a theoretical analysis of the problem:

> The traditional sociological theory of urban life implies that residence in large cities encourages greater tolerance and universalism (Wirth 1938; Simmel 1957; Park 1952). Wirth lists "toleration of differences" among the hypothesized effects of dense and heterogeneous settlements. This, together with effects such as "impersonality," "rationality," evaluating others according to their "utility," and the breakdown of "traditional base of solidarity," generates the theory that urbanism encourages the development of universalistic attitudes.
>
> Deducible from this theory is the hypothesis that *the more urban a person's place of residence (defined demographically), the more likely he is to be tolerant of racial and ethnic differences* (particularly in regard to decisions calling for universalistic criteria) (Fischer, 1971, p. 847).

(4) from a study of the occurrence of lynching in southern communities, a statement of theory and hypothesis:

> In his (1967:159) book, *Toward a Theory of Minority-Group Relations*, Hubert Blalock derives a clear and unequivocal prediction of the nature of the relation of "*symbolic* or ritualisitic forms of violence, such as lynching" to the proportion of Negroes in a community. I shall not attempt to recapitulate his argument here, but he sees such violence as one response to a perceived "power-threat" by the subordinate group. Such responses, he argues (1967:109-133, 150-160), should be positively related *with increasing slope* to the proportion of the population which belongs to the minority group, in this case to the proportion black. He produces much qualitative and some quantitative evidence to support this prediction, but observes that "certain methodological difficulties have prevented me from obtaining definitive results" from data on lynching (1967:159, 161-173). This paper reports an attempt to dispose of these difficulties, and to test his prediction (Reed, 1972, p. 356).

(2) Method

In the method section of a research report, the investigator usually reports important characteristics of his sample and the method by which it has been drawn. Also presented in this section is a description of the instruments and measures employed in the data collection phase of the study. In experimental research, the researcher must describe his experimental procedure, including the manipulation of the independent variables as well as the measurement of the dependent variable. As a final task, some instructors also ask their students to review and justify their use of tools of data analysis, including tables, statistics, and computer processing.

The following excerpts illustrate some of the central concerns of the method section:

(1) from a content analysis of the underground press, a description of the sampling strategy:

> To obtain a representative sample of underground newspapers, the following most widely circulated periodicals were selected from major centers of recent hippie activities including both eastern and western regions: Avatar (Boston), Distant Drummer (Philadelphia), East Village Other (New York), Los Angeles Free Press, San Francisco Oracle, and Washington Free Press. A single issue of each Underground Press Syndicate periodical from every second month in the period from September 1967 to August 1968 was selected on a random basis. Every second nonfictional article appearing in this sample of issues, excluding poetry and letters to the editor, was subjected to analysis (N=316).
>
> To provide a comparable sample of articles representative of middle-class values, an analysis was also conducted of concurrently published issues of the READER'S DIGEST, selected for its variety of middle class articles from diverse sources (see Ginglinger, 1955:56-61). Excluding fiction and poetry, each article appearing in every other issue of READER'S DIGEST was studied (N=162) (Levin and Spates, 1970, p. 65).

(2) from a secondary analysis of neighborliness in public housing projects, a description of measures:

> Neighborhood orientation was operationally defined along two dimensions: (1) behaviorally, as manifested by self-reported borrowing among project tenants ("Do you ever borrow from other tenants in this building?"), and (2) attitudinally, as expressed satisfaction with other project residents ("How do you feel about the tenants in this project?"). In addition, a summary index of orientation toward the public housing environment was constructed by "pair-comparing" responses to the open-ended question: "What in general is your feeling about public housing?" (Taube and Levin, 1971, p. 536).

(3) from an experimental study of displaced aggression, the description of the experimental procedure:

> Sixty male undergraduate students from an introductory psychology class at the U. of Texas (Austin) served as subjects and were randomly assigned to one of four conditions. The experiment was a 2 × 2 factorial design, with two levels of frustration-generated aggression (low versus high) and two targets for aggression (direct versus displaced).

When a subject arrived for the experiment, he was told that the experiment involved two persons and that his partner had not yet arrived. The subject was then asked to wait in the corridor outside the laboratory until the other subject arrived. During his wait it was necessary for the subject to stand and there were no chairs in the corridor. In the low-frustration condition, the subject had to wait in this position for only 5 minutes, while, in the high-frustration condition, the subject had to wait for 30 minutes (Holmes, 1972, p. 298).

(4) from a mail questionnaire study of women dentists, a description of the procedure for data collection:

In 1968, a questionnaire was mailed to women dentists, professionally inactive and active. The potential respondents were initially drawn from the 1967 Directory of the American Dental Association, using feminine-sounding first names as a basis for selection. Other names were obtained from lists furnished by the Association of American Women Dentists and the Sorority of Women Dentists. Additions were also made from names of women dentists given by respondents who answered the questionnaire. Those who wrote back that they were men and those reported as deceased were eliminated, leaving a total of 1,588 as the estimated number of women dentists. Two hundred and five questionnaires were returned by the post office, presumably because the addressees had moved. To all others, if the questionnaire was not returned as a result of the first mailing, a follow-up letter and a second copy of the questionnaire were sent. If the questionnaire was still not returned, a third letter, without a questionnaire, was sent. In total, 803 questionnaires were completed and returned (Linn, 1971, pp. 393-394).

(3) Results

In this section, the student reports the findings obtained from his research, including those in tabular or statistical form. The excerpts below illustrate divergent approaches that have been used for this purpose:

(1) from a survey of racial attitudes, a description of findings:

The extent to which whites and nonwhites endorsed the strongest integration alternative, and the average scores on the Segregation Index, have already been presented in Table 1. All differences between the two groups are statistically significant.

Both groups give high support to the notion that Negroes and whites should attend the same schools, and both are unlikely to move "if people of a different race moved next door." However, on the issue of housing, there is a great difference between item 5 and items 6 and 7. There is a sharp decrease in the percentage of whites endorsing the item when the alternative is changed to "many" people of a different race in the neighborhood. The percentage of whites who favor passage of an open housing law is even lower. (Levy, 1972, pp 225-226).

(2) from a content analysis of stereotyping in magazine ads, a statement of major results:

The occupational distribution of Negroes and whites is summarized in Table 2. While there is only a slight shift in the *above skilled labor* category of whites from 1949-50 to 1967-68, there is a major shift in the *above skilled labor* category of Negroes, from 6.1 per cent in 1949-1950 to 71.3 per cent in 1967-68. The stereotyping of Negroes as maids, cooks, servants, waiters, porters, butlers, and chauffeurs decreased from about 75 percent of all general advertisements with Negroes in 1949-50 to approximately 8 per cent in 1967-68 (Cox, 1969-70, p 604).

(3) from an experimental study of the effect of attitude similarity on heterosexual attraction, a presentation of results:

Scores for the randomly matched subjects were excluded, and the remaining data were analyzed in a $2 \times 2 \times 2$ analysis of variance (Sex of Subject $\times$ Similarity $\times$ Attitude). Two significant main effects were obtained. Female subjects tended to be more attracted to their partners than male subjects ($F = 4.56, df = 1/308, p < .05$), and more attraction was associated with similar attitudes when compared to dissimilar attitudes ($F = 63.99, df = 1/308, p < .001$) (Touhey, 1972, p 9).

(4) Discussion

The final section of the research report generally includes a discussion of the results in the light of the hypotheses of the study. It is in this section of the report that relevant implications of the research are drawn out for the reader.

The following excerpts from research reports illustrate some of the important functions of this section:

(1) from a questionnaire survey of parental educational differences and the college plans of youth, a discussion of results that contradict previous research:

While the work of Ellis and Lane and Krauss has supported the hypothesis that young people from families where the mother's education exceeds that of the father are more likely to have college plans than those from families where the father's education exceeds that of the mother, the evidence from the present study contradicts this hypothesis. In addition to demonstrating the absence of this relationship, the foregoing analysis lends a good deal of support to the opposite hypothesis, namely, that in families where the father's education is greater than that of their wives, proportionately more children plan on college than in families where mothers have more education than their husbands. (Pavalko and Walizer, 1969, pp 86-87).

(2) from a content analysis of values in youth counter culture, identification of methodological weaknesses and a suggestion for future research—

A second interpretation of the present results is also feasible, however. This would be that the very stability of major socio-cultural values implies that when they change, they do so very slowly. If this is true, it is equally possible that the prophesized change toward an expressive set of values—what Reich has called the "Greening of America"—may indeed be under way, but that the present sample was unable to detect such a shift because of (a) the nearness in time of the two periods sampled and (b) the inability of literature as a cultural indicator to reflect such a shift quickly. Such an alternative interpretation of results suggests that another analysis of the dominant culture's value structure conducted at a later time might reveal that this change had occurred (or was occurring) (Spates and Levin, 1972, p 351).

(3) from an experiment in social comparison, support for a theoretical position:

The results of this experiment support influence theory. It has been shown that once an individual is satisfied with the validity of his opinion (and thus freed of the need for social comparison), there is activated a desire to demonstrate the ability to influence other people. This ability is demonstrated by convincing others that your opinion is correct. The greater the opinion descrepancy and the more invalid the group's opinion, the greater is the perceived possibility of influence, and therefore, the greater the desire to affiliate (Gordon, 1966, p 64).

Exercises

1) Examine social science journals which contain reports of research. For several appropriate journal articles, determine how the background, method, results, and discussion of research are reported, and write a brief summary statement of each section.

REFERENCES

Ackoff, R.L. *The Design of Social Research* (Chicago: University of Chicago Press, 1953).

Becker, H.S. "Problems in the Publication of Field Studies," in A. Vidich, J. Bensman, and M. Stein (eds.), *Reflections on Community Studies* (New York: John Wiley, 1964), pp 267–284.

Bonjean, C., R. Hill, and D. McLemore. *Sociological Measurement* (San Francisco: Chandler, 1967).

Carey, J.T. "Changing Courtship Patterns in the Popular Song," *American Journal of Sociology*, 74, 6 (May, 1969), pp 720–731.

Cox, K.K. "Changes in Stereotyping of Negroes and Whites in Magazine Advertisements," *The Public Opinion Quarterly*, XXXIII, 4 (Winter, 1969-70), pp 603–606.

Dixon, W.J. BMD-Biomedical Computer Programs No II (Los Angeles: University of California, 1970).

Durkheim, E. *Suicide* (New York: The Free Press, 1951).

Festinger, L. *A Theory of Cognitive Dissonance* (Stanford: Stanford University·Press, 1957).

Fischer, C.S. "A Research Note on Urbanism and Tolerance," *American Journal of Sociology*, 76, 5 (March, 1971), pp 847–856.

Gans, H.J. "The Famine in American Mass-Communications Research," *American Journal of Sociology*, 77, 4 (January, 1972), pp 697–705.

Gordon, B.F. "Influence and Social Comparison as Motives for Affiliation," *Journal of Experimental Social Psychology*, Supplement 1 (September, 1966), pp 55–65.

Hartnagel, T.F. "Father Absence and Self Conception among Lower Class White and Negro Boys," *Social Problems*, 18, 2 (Fall, 1970), pp. 152–163.

Holmes, D.S. "Aggression, Displacement, and Guilt," *Journal of Personality and Social Psychology*, 21, 3 (1972), pp 296–301.

Lasswell, H.D. "The Structure and Function of Communication in Society," in W. Schramm (ed.), *Mass Communications* (Urbana: University of Illinois, 1960), pp 117–130.

Levin, J. *Elementary Statistics in Social Research* (New York: Harper and Row, 1973).

Levin J. and J.L. Spates, "Hippie Values: An Analysis of the Underground Press," *Youth and Society*, II, 1 (September, 1970), pp 59–73.

Levy, S.G. "Polarization in Racial Attitudes," *The Public Opinion Quarterly*, XXXVI, 2 (Summer, 1972), pp 221–234.

Linn, E.L. "Women Dentists: Career and Family," *Social Problems*, 18, 3 (Winter, 1971), pp 393–404.

Merritt, E.L. and G.J. Pyszka, *The Student Political Scientist's Handbook* (Cambridge, Mass: Schenkman, 1969).

Mitchell, William C. *Public Choice in America* (Chicago: Markham, 1971).

Namenwirth, J.Z. "Some Long- and Short-term Trends in One American Political Value: A Computer Analysis of Concern with Wealth in 62 Party Platforms," in George Gerbner, et. al. (eds.), *The Analysis of Communication Content* (New York: John Wiley, 1969), pp 223–241.

Pavalke, R.N. and M.H. Walizer, "Parental Education: Differences and the College Plans of Youth," *Sociology and Social Research*, 54, 1 (October, 1969), pp 80–89.

Phillips, B.S. *Social Research: Strategy and Tactics* (New York: Macmillan, 1971).

Reed, J.S. "Percent Black and Lynching: A Test of Blalock's Theory," *Social Forces*, 50, 3 (March, 1972), pp 356–360.

Robinson, J.P., J.G. Rusk, and K.B. Head, *Measures of Political Attitudes* (Ann Arbor: Institute for Social Research, 1968).

Rosnow, R.L., R.F. Holz, and J. Levin, "Differential Effects of Complementary and Competing Variables in Primacy-Recency," *Journal of Social Psychology*, 69, 1966, pp 135–147.

Social Science Research Council, Committee on Historiography, Bulletin 64, *The Social Sciences in Historical Study* (New York: Social Science Research Council, 1954).

Spates, J.L. and J. Levin, "Beats, Hippies, the Hip Generation, and the American Middle Class: An Analysis of Values," *International Social Science Journal*, XXIV, 2, 1972, pp 326–353.

Spilerman, S. "The Causes of Racial Disturbances: A Comparison of Alternative Explanations," *American Sociological Review*, 35, 4 (August, 1970), pp 627–649.

Taube, G. and J. Levin, "Public Housing as Neighborhood: The Effect of Local and Non-Local Participation," *Social Science Quarterly*, 52, 3 (December, 1971), pp 534–542.

Touhey, J.C. "Comparison of Two Dimensions of Attitude Similarity on Heterosexual Attraction," *Journal of Personality and Social Psychology*, 23, 1 (July, 1972), pp 8–10.

Van Dyke, V. *Political Science: A Philosophical Approach* (Stanford: Stanford University, 1960).

Webb, E.J., et. al. *Unobtrusive Measures: Nonreactive Research in the Social Sciences* (Chicago: Rand McNally, 1966).

APPENDIX A: THE USE OF COMPUTERS TO PROCESS DATA

by
Gerald S. Ferman

Computers can frequently be used to carry out an analysis more quickly and with greater accuracy than is possible by hand manipulation or calculating machine. A basic requirement for the use of computers in most of social science research is that verbal data (for example, survey responses) must be capable of being meaningfully represented by a series of numbers (that is, the numerical system representing verbal data must share essential characteristics with that data). When this requirement is satisfied, it becomes possible to employ computer software in processing data.

What is computer software? *Software* refers to canned or packaged computer programs; that is, to a set of computer programs that share certain characteristics and can be 'set-up' or activated on a data file by recording characteristics of the file in specified positions on IBM cards (or other media e.g. magnetic tapes). These programs, generally referenced by the name of the package (and a particular specification for each program in the package), can perform a variety of operations on the data. In the 'write-up' (the instructions for each program) these operations—many optional—as well as the programs limitations are specified.

Computer software programs can be compared in some critical respects to automatic washing machines; these machines are 'programmed' to automatically perform a variety of washing operations. The housewife places the laundry (equivalent to the data) in the appropriate receptacle, specifies which program options she wants performed on the laundry (e.g., cold or hot water, fast or slow agitation of the rotator) and, in some machines, indicates critical characteristics of the laundry, (e.g., its approximate weight or primary fabric element). Software programs, however, generally require more specification about the data than the analogy implies.

General Specifications for BMD Computer Software

Is it necessary to know a computer language to use a software program? Many students believe they must take a course in computer language before they can competently use software programs. This is totally incorrect, since software program write-ups can be easily understood by the average student. He need not learn a technical and specialized language to benefit from the tremendous capabilities of computers.

In the first place, the user must select and reference (call) a software package. Three useful social science oriented software packages are generally available at large computer centers: BMD, OSIRIS and SPSS. However, since the BMD package is also generally available at moderate size computer centers, only BMD will be discussed here.

System Cards-Front: Software Package, Program Identification

The number of system cards required, their content and layout (specification) vary from one computer center to another. These particulars, however, are always readily available to users. In general, when using software packages, the user must indicate the following information on these cards: the package name (in this case BMD), his name, the designation of the data file *if* the data are read from magnetic tapes or discs, and the designation of the particular software program (in the package) that he wants to use. The latter specification, of course, depends on the type of analysis desired. If, for example, contingency tables are desired, a program producing this type of output is called forth.

The specifications noted below are those required at *Western Illinois University.* *

Each row (beginning at the margin) represents *one* IBM card. The column numbers represent the respective columns on an 80 column IBM

---

* In this discussion, in order to distinguish in the card set-up a capital O from a zero, the former appears as a zero with a slashed line through it (Ø).

1	2	3	4	5	6	7	8	9	10	11	12	13	14	15	16	17	18	19	20
/	/		J	Ø	B		B	M	D		E	7	1	5	5	5	2	0	

21	22	23	24	25	26	27	28	29	30	31	32	33	34	35	36	37	38	39	40	41	42	...	80
N	A	M	E	=	(	F	E	R	M	A	N	)		T	A	P	E	=	P	S	I		

1	2	3	4	5	6	7	8	9	10	11	12	13	14	15	16	17	18	19	20	...	80
/	/		E	X	E	C		B	M	D	O	8	D								

card. It is essential that the appropriate letter or number appear in the correct (specified) column.

System Cards-Front contain the following information:

First System Card

a) JØB BMD (columns four through ten skipping seven). This instructs the computer to get ready to use one of the BMD programs in a *job* (analysis/computer run).

b) The class account number (columns twelve through nineteen). In this way a record is kept of the amount of computer time used by each class and each department.

c) NAME = and the student's name (columns twenty-one on until the name is completely punched and the parenthesis closed). This information makes it possible for the computer operator to return processed (completed) jobs to the appropriate researcher.

d) TAPE=PSI (one column skipped from the last column punched). This specification informs the computer operator that the job is to process data from a magnetic tape designated as PSI. (Important—if the job is to succeed the operator must know which tape to mount on the appropriate machine [tape drive]. If the data is not on tape, the specification [TAPE=PSI or another tape name] is not included. Thus, if the data is on IBM cards, the last specification for this first system card is the researcher's name enclosed in parentheses.)

Second System Card

e) EXEC BMDO8D (columns four through fourteen, with column eight skipped). This information instructs the computer to execute bi-medical program number O8D.

(Remember to punch the two slashed/slanted lines in columns 1 and 2 on each of these cards. They are essential.)

Problem Card

This card generally provides the following information to the program referenced/called:

a) The word PROBLEM—This tells the program that this is the Problem card.
b) The *name* of the job or researcher.
c) Whether the forthcoming data is to be read from IBM cards or some other media (e.g., magnetic tape).
d) The *number of observations* or respondents in the study.
e) The number of variables studied (e.g., questions).
f) The *kind of processing or analysis* the researcher requires; that is, the program options the researcher wants executed on the data (e.g., mean standard deviation or both).
g) The number of variables *labelled*; that is, assigned names printed in the print-out (the output of the computer analysis).
h) The number of *format cards*; that is, the number of IBM cards needed to identify the *positions* of the variables on the data cards, or tape etc.

The example below illustrates these general properties of the problem card (see bottom of page 94 and top of page 95).

BMDO8D Problem Card (the specifications of the Problem Card unique to this program are not included).

Format Card

Another general feature of BMD programs is the Format card. This card tells a program where the data is to be found on IBM cards (or card images on magnetic tape etc.). An IBM card has 80 columns and twelve rows. Data may be punched throughout the card. A program needs to know where to find the data the researcher wants it to process. The BMD Manual notes:

The word 'format' usually refers to the arrangement of information key-punched on a card. The format of a data card is a sequence of fields (variables), each of

```
1  2  3  4  5  6  7  8  9  10 11 12 13 14 15 16 17 18 19 . . .
P  R  O  B  L  M  C  R  S  T  A  B  0  0  2  0  0  5  0
```

(A)	(B)	(E)	(D)
	Short for cross tabulation – name of job	Number of Variables (or questions)	Number of Respondents

28	29	30	31	32	69	70	71	72 . . .
0	0	2	0	1	0	0	0	1
(G)			(F)		(C)		(H)	

(G)	(F)	(C)	(H)
Number of Variables labelled	This designation tells the program to exercise the contingency table option, (i.e., produce all possible two variable contingency tables).	This tells the program that data is to be read from IBM cards.	Number of Variable Format Cards

which occupies one or more columns. For the computer programs a format is a set of specifications according to which information is read [in] . . . . The specifications tell the program which parts (or columns) of the card to skip, which parts to regard as all one number, and which parts to regard as several numbers in a row. For instance, it is the format which tells the program whether a card punched '345890021' is to be read in as '34.5 89.0, .021' or '34.,9002.1' . . . (Dixon, 1970, p. 22).

Two types of format statements are alternately used in BMD programs: the F-type and the I-type.

F-Type Format   This format type is required when a decimal point is keypunched on a data card or placed/*imposed* on data when it is read into a program.

General form: 'NFW.D'

F, indicates that this is an F format (floating-point or a format that can handle decimal points); N, the number of fields/variables back to back of a given width, W (includes sign and decimal point if punched); and D, the number of digits to be placed to the right of the decimal point. D is ignored if a decimal point is punched. If N is not specified it is assumed to be 1.

An example will clarify this format procedure and introduce the skip-space technique. The variables are per-capita income and percent urbanization of fifty nations. They are placed on IBM cards in the following way. (Remember that each line represents one IBM data card)

1	2	3	4	5	6	7	8	9	10	11	12 . . .
0	1		1	0	0	1		5	0	9	
0	2		1	5	0	0		6	5	4	
0	3		8	7	5			3	0	9	
0	4		5	0	0			7	0	5	
0	5		2	0	1			0	9	3	
.			.					.			
.			.					.			
.			.					.			
5	0		2	0	1			0	9	3	

Columns one and two contain the identification number assigned to each nation; three through seven, the respective nation's per-capita income; and nine through eleven, percent urbanization. The researcher wants the 'card-reader' to skip over the identification numbers and read the two research variables. The F format card is as follows:

```
1  2  3  4  5  6  7  8  9  10 11 12 13 14 15 16 17 18 19...
(  T  4  ,  F  4  .  0  ,  T  9  ,  F  3  .  1  )
```

(Note the positions of parentheses, commas and periods—they are essential and must be punched in the appropriate columns.)

'T' instructs the card-reader to skip to the column specified—in this case, column four. In column four the card-reader is instructed to read a variable that is four columns long/wide (F4), and has no decimal point (.0). It then skips to column nine (T9), and reads another variable, three columns wide (F3) with one decimal point (.1). The following are the numbers the card-reader has placed in the memory of the computer.

1001.	50.9
1500.	65.4
875.	30.9
500.	70.5
.	.
.	.
.	.
201.	9.3

Note the placement of the decimal point on the second variable. It should be clear to the reader how the decimal point was 'imposed' on this non-decimal punched variable.

I-Type Format   This format is required for some BMD and other programs designed to process only integer values/numbers; that is, whole numbers— numbers without decimal points. The specification is 'NIW', where I indicates an I format; N, the number of fields/variables back to back (assumed to be one if not punched); and W, the width of the field (includes signs if punched). The following I format card would instruct the card-reader to read the data in the preceding example. (Note the different arrangement of the numbers.)

```
1  2  3  4  5  6  7  8  9  10 11 12 13 14 15 16...
(  T  4  ,  I  4  ,  T  9  ,  I  3  )
```

The pairs of numbers below would be stored in the computer's 'memory'.

1001	509
1500	654
875	309
500	705
.	.
.	.
.	.
201	93

Note: there are no decimal points—even to the extreme right of the numbers—whereas with the F format there are always decimal points. Below are some examples of F and I formats.

Punched Number	Format Specification		Number Stored In Memory
4521	F4.0		4521.
3525	F4.2		35.25
3515	2F2.0	(Two variables back to back)	35. 15.
3515	2F2.1		3.5 1.5
3212	I4		3212
3	I1		3
31	2I1	(Two variables back to back)	3 1
31	I2		31

Labels Card

Labels cards are used to assign names to variables. (Number designations are automatically assigned by the *order in which variables are read* into the computer's memory [i.e., the first variable specified on a format card is designated as variable 1, the second variable 2 . . .]). Every time a labelled variable is reported in the program output, e.g., the *print-out* (i.e., the printed result of the program manipulations) it will be referenced by its number and assigned name. The arrangement of the labels card is the same for all BMD programs. It is 'set-up' in the following way:

Columns	1-6	LABELS
Columns	7-10	The number of the variable to be named/ labeled. As noted, the first variable read in a format statement is variable one, the second, variable two, etc.

Columns   11-16   The name/label.

Columns   17-20   The number of the second variable to be named/labeled.

Columns   21-26   The name/label.

This format continues to column 76. This permits the researcher to label up to seven variables per label card. The following example illustrates the procedure.

Format Card

Variable Number (automatically assigned)

one   two   three   four and five (back to back)

(T9, 15, T20, 11, T30, 12, T40, 211)

The objective is to label variables one and two. (Note: all variables read in to a program need not be labelled.)

```
1 2 3 4 5 6 7 8 9 10 11 12 13 14 15 16 17 18 19 20 21 22 23 24 25 26 ... 80
L A B E L S 0 0 0  1  P  C  I  N  C  E  0  0  0  2  P  T  U  R  B  N
```

PCINCE = per-capita income
PTURBN = percent Urban

Transgeneration Card

Transgeneration cards allow the user to generate new variables from existing variables (i.e., variables read into the computer's memory). The BMD Users Manual notes:

> The term transgeneration is used to include transformations of input variables and creation of new variables prior to the normal computations performed by the various programs. (Dixon, 1970, p. 15).

Suppose a user wanted to study population density of the American states, but could only find area and population (for a given year). By using this card he could generate the variable population density (i.e., population divided by area), without erasing (removing) from the computer's memory the original variables.

This card, as the Labels card, is set-up (prepared) in the same way for all BMD programs. The following are its specifications:

Columns	1-6	TRNGEN

Columns   7-9   Variable Index k, that is, the variable number of the 'new' or 'transgenerated' variable. If three variables were read into the program (computer memory) in an analysis (computer 'run'), the first 'new' or transgenerated variable would be variable number four.

Columns   10-11   Transgeneration Code. This code value tells the program what kind of transgeneration is required, e.g., addition, division, multiplication, square rooting. (A list of code values of the kinds of transgenerations generally used by students is provided below.)

Columns   12-14   Variable index i. The subscripts used in the list of transgeneration operations below clarify this subscript and the next two.

Columns   15-20   Variable index j, or constant c.

List of Code Values and Operations. (Note that all codes cannot be used in all BMD Programs.)

Code	Operation
08	$X_i + C = X_k$
09	$X_i C = X_k$
11	$X_i + X_j = X_k$
12	$X_i - X_j = X_k$
13	$X_i - X_j = X_k$
14	$X_i / X_j = X_k$

(Codes 82,83,84,85.—are variable stacking codes for BMD 08D. These codes are used in profile analysis. For details see the complete BMD 08D write-up.)

An example will illustrate these operations:

Format (T4, F9.0, T15, F5.0)

The *first* variable designated by the format is 'total county earned income', the *second* 'county population'. The objective is to create a 'new' variable—'per capita county earned income'.

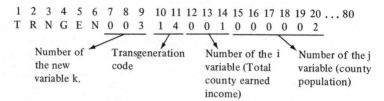

Assume that there are only three counties in the study (three data cards). The program after the transgeneration card is read would store three values for each county: the first two read in from the data cards and the third transgenerated from the first two. The diagram below shows the transgeneration operation.

Card Number	Data Card Values (Variables 1 and 2)		Transgeneration Operation (Variable 3)
	(I)	(J)	(K)
1	10000000.	2000.	(10000000./2000.) = 5000.
2	40000000.	10000.	(40000000./10000.) = 4000.
3	100000000.	20000.	(100000000./20000.) = 5000.

System Cards—Back

These cards tell the computer that the program has been read and executed (i.e., the job is finished). The computer responds by 'moving on' to the next job. As the 'front' system cards the specifications of these cards vary from one computer center to another. The following are the specifications used at Western Illinois University.

```
1  2  3  4  5  6   7  8  9   10 11 12 13 14 15 ...
F  I  N  I  S  H
/  &
```

(In columns 1-6 on the first card FINISH is punched and on the second card, in columns one and two, a slash and ampersand.)

Description of a BMD Program

A BMD program especially appropriate for student research is reviewed in this section. Because of space-limitations, all the options and specifications of the program are not included.

Illustration of Limitation Two

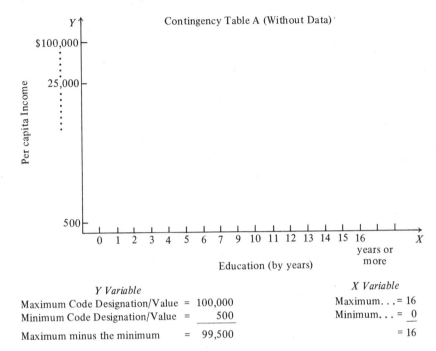

Contingency Table A (Without Data)

	Y Variable		X Variable	
Maximum Code Designation/Value	=	100,000	Maximum. . . =	16
Minimum Code Designation/Value	=	500	Minimum. . . =	0
Maximum minus the minimum	=	99,500	=	16

BMD08D—Cross Tabulation with Variable Stacking

General Description This program computes two-way frequency tables (contingency tables) of data input. These tables are computed from specified ranges of the original variables, variables after transgeneration, stacked variables (profile analysis) or combinations of these. Chi square values and degrees of freedom are calculated for each table. In addition the mean and standard deviation of each variable, and the Pearson Correlation Coefficient for each pair of variables is computed.

Limitations 1—The number of cases (e.g., observations, respondents) cannot exceed 1600.

2—The range of each variable to be cross-tabulated is restricted in the following way: The *maximum* code value of variable X minus its *minimum* code value, must be equal to or smaller than 34 but not smaller than one $(1 \leq \text{Max } X - \text{Min } X \leq 34)$, and the maximum code value of variable Y minus the minimum code value of Y must be equal to or smaller than 99 but not smaller than one (1 Max Y − Min Y ≤ 99), where X and Y are the variables on the abscissa (horizontal axis of a contingency table) and the ordinate (vertical axis) respectively.

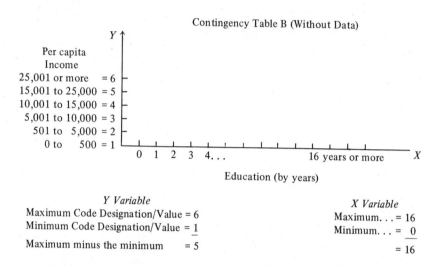

Contingency Table B (Without Data)

Per capita Income	
25,001 or more	= 6
15,001 to 25,000	= 5
10,001 to 15,000	= 4
5,001 to 10,000	= 3
501 to 5,000	= 2
0 to 500	= 1

Education (by years)

Y Variable		*X Variable*	
Maximum Code Designation/Value = 6		Maximum... = 16	
Minimum Code Designation/Value = 1		Minimum... = 0	
Maximum minus the minimum = 5		= 16	

Explanation of Tables

In contingency Table A, note the maximum and minimum code designations/values. Because the maximum code value of variable Y (per-capita income—$100,000) minus the minimum yields a number larger than 99, the program will not run, that is, it will 'bounce' or cancel out. (Limitation two has been partially violated.) In Table B the Y variable has been recoded in a way consistent with the Y variable limitation in this program (maximum [6] minus the minimum [1] of Y = 5 [a number less than 99]). The same procedure holds for the X variable with the exception that the maximum code designation minus the minimum cannot be greater than 34. Thus it should be clear that one of the cross-tabulated variables can have a range designation value from 0 to 99 (i.e. maximum minus minimum can equal any value from 0 to 99), whereas the other, from 0 to 34. Contingency Table C reflects this optimal situation.

3—The maximum frequency for any cell in the contingency table is 999. (Description of the program's Problem and Ranges cards will clarify the first two limitations.)

Order of Cards

A.	2 System Cards-Front
B.	1 Problem Card
C.	Ranges Card(s)
D.	Labels Card(s)
E.	I-Type Format Card(s)
F.	Data Cards—(Place *data* here if data is to be read from cards.)
G.	Transgeneration Card(s)
H.	2 System Cards-Back

(A parenthesis indicates that the respective card follows the general [standard] specifications reviewed in the last major section.)

Card Preparations (Specific for this Program)

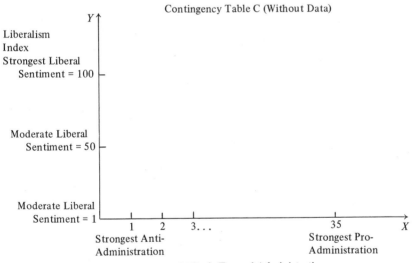

Contingency Table C (Without Data)

Y axis: Liberalism Index
Strongest Liberal Sentiment = 100
Moderate Liberal Sentiment = 50
Moderate Liberal Sentiment = 1

X axis: 1, 2, 3..., 35
Strongest Anti-Administration
Strongest Pro-Administration

Attitude Toward Administration
Index Score

Y Variable		*X Variable*	
Maximum Code Designation/Value = 100		Maximum. . . = 35	
Minimum Code Designation/Value = 1		Minimum. . . = 1	
Maximum minus the minimum	99		34

A. System Cards—Front (at Western Illinois University)

1	2	3	4	5	6	7	8	9	10	11	12	13	14	15	16	17	18	19	20
/	/		J	Ø	B		B	M	D		E	7	1	5	5	5	2	0	

21	22	23	24	25	26	27	28	29	30	31	32	33	34	35	36	37	38	39	40	41	42...80
N	A	M	E	=	(	F	E	R	M	A	N	)		T	A	P	E	=	P	S	I

1	2	3	4	5	6	7	8	9	10	11	12	13	14	15	16	17	18	19	20...80
/	/		E	X	E	C		B	M	D	O	8	D						

Remember that the designation TAPE=PS1 is included only if the data studied is to be read from the magnetic tape labelled or designated as PS1. If data is read from another tape its label is punched after the equal (=) sign. If data is read from IBM cards the last specification on the first system card is the closing parenthesis after the researcher's name. (If this point is not thoroughly understood return to "System Cards Front . . . First System Card" in this Appendix).

B. Problem Card

Columns	1-6	PROBLM
Columns	7-12	Job name or researcher's name abbreviated (if necessary) to fit in these six columns.
Columns	13-15	Number of variables.

For instance, if the study consists of two questions, 002 is punched.

| Columns | 16-19 | Number of cases or observation (e.g., respondents). |

There are 1557 respondents in the 1968 Institute for Social Research (University of Michigan) Election Study. A student examining this data, therefore, would punch 1557 in these columns.

| Columns | 20-22 | Leave blank/skip. |
| Columns | 23-25 | Number of variables added to the original set (i.e., the number of variables transgenerated). |

If two 'new' variables are transgenerated, 002 would be punched. If no variables are transgenerated, the columns are left blank.

| Columns | 26-27 | Leave blank/skip. |

Columns   28-30   Number of variables labelled.
If no variables are labelled the columns are left blank.

Columns   31-32   Place 01 (zero, one) in these columns;.
This instructs the program to compute and print all possible combinations of two-way contingency tables; that is, every variable will be cross-tabulated against every other variable in the study.

Columns   33-36   Leave blank/skip.

Columns   67-68   Number of transgeneration cards.
If two variables are transgenerated there would be two transgeneration (TRNGEN) cards—002 would be punched.

Columns   69-70   If data is read from IBM cards, 00 is punched. If data is read from another device (e.g., a magnetic tape), the number or code designation of the device is punched. (At Western Illinois University, for the 1968 Election Study, 09 [the designation of the appropriate tape device/drive] is punched.)

Columns   71-72   Number of format cards.
Generally, the student researcher will use only one format card—thus 01 is punched.

C. Ranges-Card(s) This card tells the program the absolute values of the maximum and minimum code designations of each variable. For example, for the following survey question the values are eight (maximum) and zero (minimum):

How do you feel about zoning regulations?

      8 Strongly Support
      6 Support
      4 Not Sure
      2 Against
      0 Strongly Against

The program uses these values to set the range of the axes of the contingency table/graph. The card is prepared in the following way:

Columns   1-6   RANGES

Columns   7-12   Maximum value of variable one.

Columns   13-18   Minimum value of variable one.

Columns   19-24   Maximum value of variable two.

Columns   25-30   Minimum value of variable two.
This pattern—six columns for maximum and six columns for minimum—continues until all the variables (including any 'new' or transgenerated variables) are specified (if less than five), or five variables are specified (i.e., to column 66). If there are more than five variables in the study, a second card is keypunched in the same manner (more than 10, a third etc.). For example, if the study included two questions (variables) with the range values as the question above, the card would be keypunched with the following values:

```
1 2 3 4 5 6 7 8 9 10 11 12 13 14 15 16 17 18 19 20 21 22 23 24 25 26 27 28 29 30. . .80
R A N G E S 0 0 0  0  0  8  0  0  0  0  0  0  0  0  0  0  0  8  0  0  0  0  0  0  0
```

D. and E. Data Cards and Format Card—Student Generated Data If a student collects data it may be keypunched on IBM cards in almost any arrangement (configuration) the researcher desires. However, because this program requires an I-format, there is one restriction; the researcher cannot punch decimal points on data cards. (If decimal points are already punched, the format card must be written so that they are not read into the program.) For This program the format card and data cards for a two variable study could be set-up in the following way:

(Assume a study codebook identifying the variables, code values and their locations/positions on the data cards, is provided. See the BMD08D illustration below and/or Appendix C if the idea and content of a codebook is not understood.)

I-Format for Dummy Data

Card
Number

	1	2	3	4	5	6	7	8	9	10	11	12	13	14	15	16 ...
1	(	T	4	,	2	I	1	)								

Card   Data Cards
Number

	1	2	3	4	5	6	7	8	9	10	11	12	13 ...
1	0	1		2	1								
2	0	2		4	4								
3	0	3		3	1								
•													
•													
50	5	0		1	3								

(The values in columns one and two – not read into the program – list the identification number of each card.)

Project Generated Data A student using project generated data—for instance, the part of the 1968 election study referenced in Appendix C—would instruct the program to read the data desired by referring to the notations in the Study Codebook. A study codebook lists the items (in the above case, questions); their code values, that is the numbers assigned to the various responses; and the columns in which the respective coded answers/responses are punched. For example, the following format statement instructs the program to read the education and religion variables (column 15 and 20-21), respectively, using information from the codebook illustrated below:

```
1  2  3  4  5  6  7  8  9  10 11 12 13 14 15 16
(  T  1  5  ,  I  1  ,  T  2  0  ,  I  2  )
```

Codebook – 1976 Pre-Election Survey Questions

Column	*Code Values*	*Questions*
.	.	.
.	.	.
.	.	.
15		How many years of formal education did you complete?
	1. 5 or less years	
	2. 5.1 to 10 years	
	3. 10.1 to 15 years	
	4. 15.1 to 20 years	
16		What is your sex?
	1. Male	
	2. Female	
.		
.		
.		
20-21		What is your religion?
	10. Protestant	
	20. Catholic	
	30. Jewish	
	40. Don't Know	
	50. No Response	

Illustration of BMD08D Job To further clarify these instructions a simple application follows.

Example One

Test Hypothesis:

The greater the education, the greater the income.

Research Task:

Cross-tabulate 'income' and 'education' of fifty respondents to a survey.

Study Codebook – Income-Education Study

Column	Code Values	Questions
1–2	Respondent's Identification Number	
4		How many years of formal education did you complete?

1. 0-5 years
2. 5.1-10 years
3. 10.1-14 years
4. 14.1-18 years
5. 18.1 or more

5		Which income category best reflects your annual income?

1. $0-4,000
2. 4,001-8,000
3. 8,001-12,000
4. 12,001-16,000
5. 16,001 or more

Card Specification (in proper order)

```
1  2  3  4  5  6  7  8  9  10 11 12 13 14 15 16 17 18 19 20
/  /     J  Ø  B     B  M  D     E  7  1  5  5  5  2  0

            21 22 23 24 25 26 27 28 29 30 31 32 33 34 35 36 37 38 39 40 ... 80
            N  A  M  E  =  (  F  E  R  M  A  N  )

1  2  3  4  5  6  7  8  9  10 11 12 13 14 15 16 17 18 19 20 ... 80
/  /     E  X  E  C     B  M  D  0  8  D

1  2  3  4  5  6  7  8  9  10 11 12 13 14 15 16 17 18 19 20 21 22 23 24 25
P  R  Ø  B  L  M  F  E  R  M  A  N  0  0  2  0  0  5  0

            26 27 28 29 30 31 32 33 ... 67 68 69 70 71 72 ... 80
            0  0  2  0  1                    0  1
```

(Thus, there are two variables (columns 13-15), fifty cases (16-19), both variables are to be labelled (28-30), all variables are to be cross-tabulated

```
1 2 3 4 5 6 7 8 9 10 11 12 13 14 15 16 17 18 19 20 21 22 23 24 25 26 27 28 29 30...80
RANGES 000 0  0 5 0 0 0 0 0 1 0 0 0 0 0 5 0 0 0 0 0 1
LABELS 000 1 E D U C T N 0 0 0 2 I N C O M E
(T 4 , 2 I 1 )
```

(The above format is more efficient than (T4, I1, I1) although this will work.)

```
1   2   3   4   5 . . .
0   1       5   1
0   2       4   2            (Data Cards)
0   3       3   3
0   4       1   2
0   5       2   1
0   6       5   4
—
—
—
5   0       5   3
F   I   N   I   S   H
/   &
```

(31-32)(in this case one contingency table is produced), and the data is to be read from IBM cards (69-70) as specified by a single format card (71-72))

Note—Where zeros are appropriate the column may be left blank. (A blank space is understood by the program as a zero punch.)

Sample Output of Program

```
BMD08D – CROSS TABULATION WITH VARIABLE STACKING – REVISED JUNE 26, 1969
HEALTH SCIENCES COMPUTING FACILITY, UCLA
PROBLEM CODE  .  .  .  .  .  .  FERMAN
NO. OF VARIABLES  .  .  .  .  .          2
NO. OF CASES  .  .  .  .  .  .  .        50
NO. OF TRNGEN CARD(S) .  .  .            0
NO. OF VARIABLE FORMAT CARD(S)           1


VARIABLE FORMAT CARD(S)
(T4,2I1)

        INCOME IS CROSS TABULATED WITH        EDUCTN      OR,

    VARIABLE  2 IS CROSS TABULATED WITH VARIABLE  1


    NUMBER OF REPLICATIONS=        50


    VARIABLE MAXIMUM MINIMUM  (AS SPECIFIED)
        2           5       1
        1           5       1
```

```
( 2)                      EXTREME RIGHT VALUE IS ROW TOTAL)
INCOME
    5  *          1  2  5    8
    4  *       1  3  8  1    13
    3  *          1  7  1    9
    2  *       2  8  1       11
    1  *       7  2          9
        ***********************
    ( 1)       1    3    5
   EDUCTN         2    4

   COLUMN      9   12    6
    TOTAL     12   11

   GRAND TOTAL=     50


CHI-SQUARE (OF TABLE)         87.45219
DF=      16

(THE FOLLOWING COMPUTATIONS ARE BASED ON ALL DATA AS ENTERED
EVEN IF SOME ARE EXCLUDED FROM THE ABOVE TABLE).

CORRELATION COEFFICIENT  0.8864
MEAN (   1)=      2.86000     SD(   1)=      1.29378
MEAN (   2)=      3.00000     SD(   2)=      1.37024
```

(*Note*: The second variable read into the program, income (Col. 5), is displayed on the Y or vertical axis and the first, education (Col. 4), on the X or horizontal axis. Thus the row totals reflect the distribution of income, and the column totals, education. Since the latter is the independent variable, the column totals should be read to test the hypothesis).

Thus, BMD08D prints:

a) its name and source
b) critical specifications of the problem card
c) the format card
      and, for each table,
d) the number and label of each variable
e) the number of observations in the study (replications)
f) the maximum and minimum code values
g) the contingency table (including row and column totals)
h) the total number of observations represented in the table (Grand Total)
i) the Chi-square and df of the table
j) the Correlation Coefficient, and

k) the mean and standard deviation of each of the cross-tabulated variables.

Substantively, from the evidence above, it appears reasonable to conclude that the hypothesis is more tenable than it was before the data test (i.e., people with 'higher' education appear to have higher income, and vice-versa).

Example Two

Test Hypothesis:

The political identity of fathers tends to influence that of their children. In other words, young people tend to identify with the political party of their fathers.

Research Task:

Cross-tabulate appropriate questions from the 1968 Presidential Election Study. (The questions below were selected from the codebook in Appendix C).

Column	Code Values	Questions
.	.	.
.	.	.
.	.	.
.	.	.
28		Generally speaking do you usually think of yourself as a Republican, Democrat, Independent, or what?
		1. Republican
		2. Democrat
		3. Independent
		(Note—minor party responses are not included in this example.)
31		Did he (R's father) think of himself mostly as a Democrat, as a Republican, or what?
		1. Democrat
		2. Republican
		3. Independent, shifted around

```
1 2 3 4 5 6 7 8 9 10 11 12 13 14 15 16 17 18 19 20 21 22 23 24 25 26
/ /   J Ø B   B M D       E 7 1 5 5 5 2 0     N A M E = (

27 28 29 30 31 32 33 34 35 36 37 38 39 40 41 42 43 44 . . . 80
F E R M A N )     T A P E = P S 1
```

PS1 is the designation assigned to the tape on which the 1968 Election data is stored at Western Illinois University.

1 2 3 4 5 6 7 8 9 10 11 12 13 14 15 16 17 18 19 20 21 22 23 24 25 26 . . . 80
/ / E X E C   B M D 0 8 D

1 2 3 4 5 6 7 8 9 10 11 12 13 14 15 16 17 18 19 20 21 22 23 24 25 26
P R Ø B L M F E R M   A N 0 0 2 1 5 5 7

27 28 29 30 31 32 33 . . . 69 70 71 72 . . . 80
0 0 2 0 1   0 9 0 1

Thus, there are two variables (columns 13-15); 1557 cases, that is, people interviewed in the survey (16-19); both variables are to be labelled (28-30); and every variable is to be cross-tabulated with every other variable (31-32). Furthermore, columns 69-70 indicate that the data tape is to be read from a tape-drive device machine, identified by the computer as 09. The last two columns (71-72) indicate that only one format card is necessary to specify the column location/position of the data.

1 2 3 4 5 6 7 8 9 10 11 12 13 14 15 16 17 18 19 20 21 22 23 24 25 26 27 28 29 30 . . . 80
RANGES 0 0 0 0 0 3 0 0 0 0 0 1 0 0 0 0 0 3 0 0 0 0 0 1

1 2 3 4 5 6 7 8 9 10 11 12 13 14 15 16 17 18 19 20 21 22 23 24 25 26 27 . . . 80
L A B E L S 0 0 0 1 R P T Y I D 0 0 0 2 F P T Y I D
(T 2 8 , I 1 , T 3 1 , I 1)
F I N I S H
/ &

OUTPUT OF PROGRAM

BMD08D – CROSS TABULATION WITH VARIABLE STACKING – REVISED JUNE 26, 1969
HEALTH SCIENCES COMPUTING FACILITY, UCLA
PROBLEM CODE . . . . FERMAN
NO. OF VARIABLES 2
NO. OF CASES 1557
NO. OF TRNGEN CARD(S) 0
NO. OF VARIABLE FORMAT CARD(S) 1

VARIABLE FORMAT CARD(S)
(T28,11,131,11)

FPTYIC IS CROSS TABULATED WITH   RPTYID   OR,

VARIABLE 2 IS CROSS TABULATED WITH VARIABLE 1

NUMBER OF REPLICATIONS = 1557

VARIABLE	MAXIMUM	MINIMUM	(AS SPECIFIED)
2	3	1	
1	3	1	

```
( 2)              (EXTREME RIGHT VALUE IS ROW TOTAL)
FPTYIC

  + 3 *   10 14 49      73
      2 *  226 91 87     404
      1 *   86480187     753
           * ********************

( 1)          1     3
RPTYIC            2


COLUMN  322     323
  TOTAL     585


GRAND TOTAL = 1230



CHI–SQUARE (OF TABLE)        361.19556
DF=     4


VALUES NOT ENTERED 327


(THE FOLLOWING COMPUTATIONS ARE BASED ON ALL DATA AS ENTERED
EVEN IF SOME ARE EXCLUDED FROM THE ABOVE TABLE).

CORRELATION COEFFICIENT 0.0933
MEAN ( 1) =      2.13873    SD( 1) =      0.95059
MEAN ( 2) =      2.26911    SD( 2) =      2.22371
```

(Note: The correlation coefficient is uninterpretable because of the disimilar coding of responses [Independents are coded 3 on both questions, but Democrats and Republicans, one (1) on one question and (2) on the other.])

Analysis of Contingency Table

1. Of the 753 fathers that identify with the Democratic Party, 480 of their sons or daughters identify with that party, (64%).

2. Of the 404 fathers that identify with the Republican Party, 226 of their sons or daughters identify with that party, (56%).

3. Of the 73 fathers that think of themselves as independents, 49 of their sons or daughters think of themselves as independents, (67%).

Thus, given the above spot analysis (and the clear distribution of cell values by rows) it appears reasonable to conclude that the findings tend to confirm the hypothesis.

APPENDIX B: GUIDELINES FOR USE OF THE IBM 29 CARD PUNCH

This brochure provides instructions which should make it possible for the beginner to use the IBM 29 Card Punch without additional help. Only the most fundamental use of the Card Punch is described here. As experience is gained by the user, further options available with the 29 will become evident. At that time, qualified help should be sought if necessary.

1. *Sequence of Steps in Use of the 29*: (Special Options Not Utilized)
   Before looking at this series of steps, examine Figures 1 and 2 which present an overall view of the 29 Card Punch and show keyboard details.

   a) Turn the POWER SWITCH on. (The location of the POWER SWITCH is shown in Figure 2.)

   b) Place a deck of blank cards, 9-edge down, face towards you, in the CARD HOPPER. (A typical card is shown in Figure 4. The 9-edge is

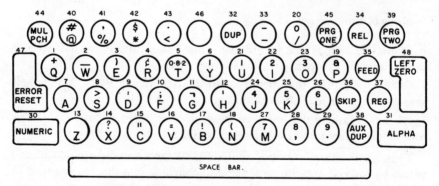

Figure 1. Detailed Diagram of the Keyboard

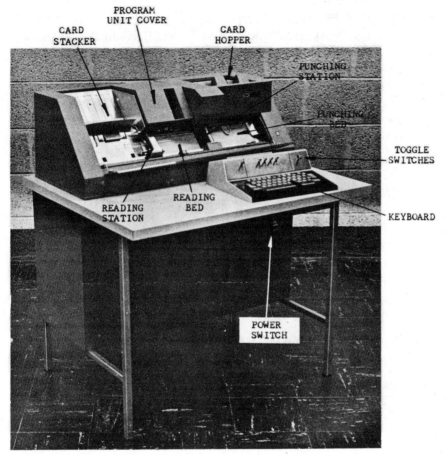

Figure 2. The IBM 29 Card Punch

the bottom edge of the card. The location of the CARD HOPPER is shown in Figure 2.)

c) Place the TOGGLE SWITCHES AUTO SKIP DUP, AUTO FEED, and PRINT in the ON position. (TOGGLE SWITCHES are shown in detail in Figure 3. Position of the TOGGLE SWITCHES PROG SEL and LZ PRINT is arbitrary. The CLEAR switch is at rest only in the CLEAR position.)

d) Push the FEED key. This causes a card to be fed down from the CARD HOPPER into the PUNCHING BED, putting it in pre-registering position. (The FEED key is Key 35 in Figure 1.)

e) Push the FEED key again. This causes another card to be fed down from the CARD HOPPER into the PUNCHING BED, and simultaneously registers the first card for punching at the PUNCHING STATION. (See Figure 2.)

f) Now key-punch the desired information, using appropriate keys at the KEYBOARD Hold down the NUMERIC key (Key 20, Figure 1) only for characters shown on the upper half of the keys. Push the Space Bar each time a card column is to be left blank.

g) When you finish punching a given card, push the REL (*rel*ease) key (Key 34, Figure 1). This causes four things to happen:

1) If a card was at the READING STATION, it moves up into the CARD STACKER.

2) The card at the PUNCHING STATION moves into the READING BED and is registered at the READING STATION.

3) The card in the PUNCHING BED is registered at the PUNCHING STATION.

4) Another card is fed from the CARD HOPPER into the PUNCHING BED, where it remains in pre-registering position.

h) Repeat Steps f) and g) unitl you are finished.

Figure 3. Detailed View of the Toggle Switches

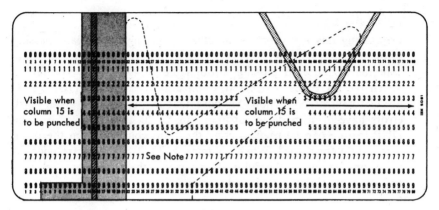

Figure 4. Card Visibility at the Punching Station

2. *Keyboard Summary*:

Each key in Figure 1 is numbered for purposes of this keyboard summary.

Punching Keys:

Keys 1 through 29, 33, and 40 through 43 are used to directly enter punches in cards. These keys can be pressed when the keyboard is in either *numeric* or *alphabetic shift* to produce either the upper or lower key character, respectively. When neither the NUMERIC Shift Key (Key 30) nor the ALPHAbetic Shift Key (Key 31) is depressed, the keyboard is automatically in alphabetic shift. (This last statement assumes that no Program Card is being used.)

Space Bar:

The Space Bar can be pressed any time a card column is to be skipped over without entering a punch into it.

Functional Keys:

30

NUMERIC (Numeric Shift)

While this key is depressed, the keyboard is shifted into numeric position (upper character position).

31

ALPHA (Alphabetic Shift)

While this key is depressed, the keyboard is shifted into alphabetic position (lower character position).

32

DUP (*Dup*licate)

Depressing this key causes characters appearing in the card passing through the READING STATION to be duplicated in corresponding columns of the card passing through the PUNCHING STATION. When the DUP key is released, duplication ceases. The DUP key is useful for error correction. Suppose that in punching a given card, errors have been made in card columns 5, 20, 21, and 32. Then the DUP feature can be used to copy the valid columns from the given card into a fresh card. When columns 5, 20, 21, and 32 are encountered, one by one, in the duplication process, the DUP key is released and the correct entries are made instead.

33

REL (*Rel*ease)

When the TOGGLE SWITCH AUTO FEED is On, pressing the REL key causes the four things listed under Step g), page 1, to occur. When AUTO FEED is Off, only the first three effects listed under Step g) take place.

35

FEED (Card Feed)

The FEED key is inactive if a card is registered at the PUNCHING STATION. Assuming no card is registered for punching, pushing the FEED key produces these effects:

1) If a card was in the READING BED, it is registered at the READING STATION.

2) If a card was in the PUNCHING BED, it is registered at the PUNCHING STATION.

3) A card is fed from the CARD HOPPER into the PUNCHING BED, where it remains in pre-registering position.

37

REG (Card *Reg*ister)

This key is used when cards are inserted manually into pre-registering position in the PUNCHING and/or READING BED, Depressing the key causes cards in those two beds to be registered at the corresponding station.

3. *Determination of Column into Which Next Punch Will be Entered*:

Figure 4 illustrates the fact that not all card columns are visible as a card moves through the PUNCHING STATION. In the example of Figure 4, card columns 13 through 21 are blocked from view when card column 15 is being punched. One easy way to establish which card column is under the punching head is to look at the COLUMN INDICATOR which can be seen through the window in the PROGRAM UNIT COVER (See Figure 2). Figure 5 shows the position of the COLUMN INDICATOR when card column 12 is the column under the punching head.

Figure 5. View of COLUMN INDICATOR as Seen Through Window in the PROGRAM UNIT COVER

4. *Program Card Preparation*:

The program unit is a device which automates certain repetitive operations that may be involved in card punching. This automatic control is accomplished by means of a program card. Description of program card preparation and use can be found in *Introduction to Data Processing*, by Arnold, Hill and Nichols, pp. 140–142.

Figure 1 courtesy of Don Danford
Figures 2, 3, 5 Courtesy Bob Kalmbach
Figure 4 Courtesy IBM*

* The authors would like to express their sincere appreciation to the University of Michigan Computer Center for permission to include this material in the present work.

APPENDIX C: 1968 PRESIDENTIAL ELECTION STUDY CODEBOOK*

Appendix C contains a 1968 Presidential Election Study codebook. In order to clarify and summarize the topics and questions of this study, the following "mini-codebook" has been included as well.

Mini-Codebook
National Sample N = 1557
Topics, Sense of the Questions, and *Codebook***
(selected questions and code values from the 1968 study)
Column
Number

1-4	Interview number

RESPONDENT'S (R's) LIVING SPACE

5	Respondent's (R's) location (Urban-Rural)
6	Region of interview
7-8	State of interview

PREDICTION & CARE ABOUT 1968 RACE

9	Does R care much who wins the presidency

---

* The data utilized in this appendix were made available (in part) by the Inter-University Consortium for Political Research. The data were originally collected by the Survey Research Center Political Behavior Program, Institute for Social Research, the University of Michigan. Neither the original collectors of data nor the Consortium bear any responsibility for the analysis or interpretation of selection of questions in the codebook presented here.
** Note that the variables (questions) are referenced in terms of their respective locations on the data cards. For example, the "region of interview" question may be referred to as the variable in column 6.

AGE

EVALUATION OF JOHNSON'S PERFORMANCE

MOST IMPORTANT NATIONAL PROBLEMS

POWER OF FEDERAL GOVERNMENT

GOVERNMENT'S ROLE IN ENSURING STANDARD OF LIVING

EFFECT OF ELECTION ON R'S FINANCIAL SITUATION (PARTY CONSIDERED)

GOVERNMENT AND PARTY ROLE IN SCHOOL INTEGRATION

CIVIL RIGHTS

NEIGHBORHOOD SEGREGATION

RACIAL STAND OF R

RACIAL MIX OF R'S ENVIRONMENT

VIETNAM WAR—ATTENTION, RIGHT OR MISTAKE, PARTY STANDS

26   Were we right in getting into Vietnam
27   Which party takes a stronger stand on Vietnam

R'S PARTY AFFILIATION: PRESENT
28   Which party does R consider self as
29   How strongly (party or independent) does R feel

R'S PARENTS: PARTY AFFILIATION & POLITICAL INTEREST
30   Was R's father very much interested in politics
31   What party did R's father think of self as

PAST PRESIDENTIAL VOTING BEHAVIOR
32   Has R always voted for the same party

1968 CAMPAIGN: VOTE INTENTION
33   Who will R vote for for President

POLITICAL EFFICACY
34   Do public officials care what people like R think
35   Is voting the only way people like R can have a say
36   Is government too complex for people like R to understand

PERSONAL DATA
37   R's marital status

FAMILY COMPOSITION
38   Number of children in R's family under 18

R's EDUCATION AND COLLEGES
39   R's educational level

R's MAIN OCCUPATION SECTION
40-41   Socio-economic status of occupation
42   R's main occupation—is R self-employed

HEAD'S MAIN OCCUPATION SECTION
43-44   Head's main occupation—Socio-economic status of occupation
45   Head's main occupation—is head self-employed

UNION MEMBERSHIP: R, HEAD, OTHER HOUSE-HOLD MEMBER
46   Does anyone in R's household belong to a union

R's CLASS IDENTIFICATION

47   Which class does R think of self as
48   What class was R's family when R was growing up

R's RELIGIOUS PREFERENCE

49-50   R's religion
51   How often does R go to church
52   What is R's opinion on the Bible

MILITARY SERVICE

53   Have any family members served in the past 6 years

"FEELING THERMOMETER"—GROUPS IN SOCIETY

54-55   Feeling thermometer—big business
56-57   Feeling thermometer—liberals
58-59   Feeling thermometer—college students
60-61   Feeling thermometer—the military
62-63   Feeling thermometer—Vietnam war protesters
64-65   Feeling thermometer—labor unions
66-67   Feeling thermometer—Negroes

R's INCOME

68-69   What will R and family's total income be this year
70   Does R own or rent R's home

SEX

71   R's sex

CONDITIONS OF THE PRE-ELECTION INTERVIEW

72   Level of R's interest in politics
73   Level of R's information about politics

R's PERSONAL FINANCIAL SITUATION: PRESENT

74   Is R and family making as much money as a year ago

PRESIDENTIAL VOTE

75   Whom did R vote for for President

OTHER STATE & LOCAL OFFICES

76   Did R vote a straight ticket for other offices

CONSERVATIVE-LIBERAL PARTY DIFFERENCES

77   Is one party more conservative than the other

SCHOOL PRAYER
78   Should prayer be allowed in public schools

PERSONAL EFFECTIVENESS & TRUST
79   How satisfying is R's life these days
80   Generally speaking, can most people be trusted

Codebook*

1-4   Interview number
5   Respondent's location (Urban-Rural)
    1. Central cities of 12 largest SMSA's (including consolidated areas)   2. Cities of 50,000 and over, exclusive of (1) 3. Urban places, 10,000–49,999 4. Urban places 2,500–9,999 and other urbanized areas not included in above codes 5. Rural, in an SMSA 6. Rural, not in an SMSA
6   Region of interview
    1. Northeast 2. Midwest 3. South 4. Far West
7-8   State of interview**
    01. Connecticut 02. Maine 03. Massachusetts 04. New Hampshire 05. Rhode Island 06. Vermont 09. General mention of area 11. Delaware 12. New Jersey 13. New York 14. Pennsylvania 18. East 19. General mention of area 21. Illinois 22. Indiana 23. Michigan 24. Ohio 25. Wisconsin 29. General mention of area 31. Iowa 32. Kansas 33. Minnesota 34. Missouri 35. Nebraska 36. North Dakota 37. South Dakota 38. Middle West 41. Alabama 42. Arkansas 43. Florida 44. Georgia 45. Louisiana 46. Mississippi 47. North Carolina 48. South Carolina 49. Texas 40. Virginia 58. General mention of south, reference to two or more states in the south 51. Kentucky 52. Maryland 53. Oklahoma 54. Tennessee 55. Washington, D.C. 56. West Virginia 59. General mention of area 61. Arizona 62. Colorado 63. Idaho 64. Montana 65. Nevada 66. New Mexico 67. Utah 68. Wyoming 71. Califor-

---

* DK = Don't Know NA = No Answer INAP. = Inappropriate
** "General Mention of Area" refers to specific regions: 10. New England 19. Middle Atlantic 29. East North Central 59. Border States 79. Pacific States

nia 72. Oregon 73. Washington 78. West 79. General mention of area 80. Alaska 81. Hawaii 82. Puerto Rico 83. American Samoa, Guam 84. Panama Canal Zone 85. Trust Territory of the Pacific Islands 86. Virgin Islands 87. Other U.S. Dependencies 92. Northeast and Midwest (N.E. or M.A. and E.N.C. or W.N.C.) 94. Far West and Midwest 95. Far West and South 96. Midwest and South 98. Lived in 3 or more regions. (NA whether lived in one more than the rest) 99. United States, NA which state

9   Generally speaking, would you say that you personally care a good deal which party wins the presidential election this fall or that you don't care very much which party wins?
       1. Care very much 2. Care, care pretty much 3. Pro-con, depends 4. Don't care very much, care a little, care some 5. Don't care at all 6. Don't care about party, only about the man 8. DK 9. NA

10-11   Actual age of respondent
        00-98. actual age 99. NA

12   In general, how do you feel about how President Johnson has done his job? Would you rate his handling of America's problems over the past four years as very good, good, fair, poor, or very poor?
       1. Very good 2. Good 3. Fair 4. Poor 5. Very poor 8. DK 9. NA

13   As you well know, the government faces many serious problems in this country and in other parts of the world. What do you personally feel are (is) the most important problems the government in Washington should try to take care of?
       0. Social welfare problems 1. Agricultural and natural resources problems 2. Labor problems, union-management relations 3. Racial and public order problems 4. Economic, business, and consumer problems 5. Foreign affairs problems (specific trouble spots, aid and military strength) 6. Foreign affairs—general (relations with U.N., Communist Block and regions) 7. National defense problems 8. Problems relating to the functioning of the government 9. Miscellaneous and missing data.

14   Some people are afraid the government in Washington is getting too powerful for the good of the country and the individual person. Others feel that the government in Washington is not getting too strong for the good of the country." Have you been interested enough in this to favor one side over the other?   (IF YES) What is your feeling, do you think—

0. No interest ("No" box checked) 1. (Yes) the government is getting too powerful 3. (Yes) other, depends, both boxes checked 5. (Yes) the government has not gotten too strong 8. DK 9 NA

15   "In general some people feel that the government in Washington should see to it that every person has a job and a good standard of living. Others think the government should just let each person get ahead on his own," Have you been interested enough in this to favor one side over the other? (IF YES) Do you think that the government—

0. No interest ("no" box checked) 1. (Yes) should see to it that every person has a job and a good standard of living 3. (Yes) other, depends, both boxes checked 5. (Yes) should let each person get ahead on his own 8. DK 9. NA

16   Do you think it will make any difference in how you and your family get along financially whether the Republicans or Democrats win the election? (IF YES) Why is that? (IF MAKES A DIFFERENCE AND NOT CLEAR WHICH PARTY WOULD BE BEST) Do you think you'll be better off or worse off financially if the Democrats win the election?

Better off if the Democrats win (worse off if the Republicans win) 0. Very important differences. Many differences. Big difference. (Mentions 3 or more differences) 1. Important differences. Some differences, NA what. (Mentions 1 or 2 differences) 2. Minor differences. Not important. Some differences but DK what they are 3. No difference. About the same

Worse off if the Democrats win (better off if the Republicans win) 4. Minor differences. Not important. Some differences but DK what they are. 5. Important differences. Some differences, NA what (Mentions 1 or 2 differences) 6. Very important differences. Many differences. Big difference.

(Mentions 3 or more differences) 7. No difference between Democrats and Republicans. Wallace would make difference, Depends. 9. Other, DK, NA

17 "Some people say that the government in Washington should see to it that white and Negro children are allowed to go to the same schools, Others claim that this is not the government's business." Have you been concerned enough about this question to favor one side over the other? _____
(IF YES) Do you think the government in Washington should—

0. No interest ("No" box checked) 1. (Yes) see to it that white and Negro children go to the same schools 3. (Yes) other, depends, both boxes checked 5. (Yes) stay out of this area as it is none of its business 8. DK 9. NA

18 Which party do you think is more likely to want the government to see to it that the white and Negro children go to the same schools?

0. INAP., coded 8 or 0 in Column 17 1. Democrats 3. No difference 5. Republicans 6. No difference in major parties, Wallace (AIP) would do what I want 8. DK 9. NA

19 Some say that the civil rights people have been trying to push too fast. Others feel they haven't pushed fast enough. How about you: Do you think that civil rights leaders are trying to push too fast, are going too slowly, or are they moving about the right speed?

1. Too fast 3. About right; pro-con 5. Too slowly 8. DK 9. NA

20 Do you think the actions Negroes have taken have, on the whole, helped their cause, or on the whole have hurt their cause.

1. Helped 2. Helped more than hurt 3. Some help, some hurt. Both boxes checked—no other response 4. Hurt more than helped 5. Hurt 8. DK 9. NA

21 Which of these statements would you agree with:

1. White people have a right to keep Negroes out of their neighborhoods if they want to. 5. Negroes have a right to live wherever they can afford to, just like anybody else 8. Don't know; depends; can't decide. Both boxes checked 9. NA

22   What about you? Are you in favor of desegregation, strict segregation, or something in between?

1. Desegregation 3. In between 5. Segregation 8. DK 9. NA

23   Is this neighborhood you now live in:

1. All white 2. Mostly white 3. About half and half 4. Mostly Negro 5. All Negro 8. DK 9. NA

24   Are your friends:

1. All white 2. Mostly white 3. About half and half 4. Mostly Negro 5. All Negro 8. DK 9. NA

25   How much attention have you been paying to what is going on in Vietnam?

1. A good deal 3. Some 5. Not much 8. DK 9. NA

26   Do you think we did the right thing in getting into the fighting in Vietnam or should we have stayed out?

1. Yes, did the right thing 3. Other; depends. Both boxes checked 5. No, should have stayed out 8. DK 9. NA

27   Which party do you think is more likely to take a stronger stand even if it means invading North Vietnam?

1. Democrats 3. No difference 5. Republicans 6. Wallace 8. DK 9. NA

28   Generally speaking do you usually think of yourself as a Republican, Democrat, independent, or what?

0. Other minor party 1. Republican 2. Democrat 3. Independent 4. No preference; against both parties; etc. 5 Liberal party 6. Conservative party 7. Refused to say 8. DK, no interest (R is apolitical) 9. NA

29   Would you call yourself a strong (R) (D) or not a very strong (R) (D)? (If independent or other) do you think of yourself as closer to the Republican or Democratic party?

The R who say he has "no preference" and is closer to neither party is coded 3 (Independent) if he seems to have some interest in politics. He is coded 8 (Apolitical) if he seems to have little interest in politics. The "minor party" identifier who is closer to neither party is coded 7 (Minor party).

0. Strong Democrat 1. Not very strong Democrat 2. Independent closer to Democrats 3. Independent 4. Independent closer to Republicans 5. Not very strong Republican

6. Strong Republican 7. Other, minor party and refused to say 8. Apolitical 9. NA

30 Do you remember when you were growing up whether your father was very much interested in politics, somewhat interested, or didn't he pay much attention to it?

  0. Father wasn't living, not raised by father , no parallel information for father surrogate 1. Very much interested 3. Somewhat interested 5. Not much attention 8. DK 9. NA

31 Did he (R's father) think of himself mostly as a Democrat, as a Republican, or what?

  0. Father wasn't living, not raised by father, no parallel information for father surrogate. Coded 0 in Column 30, 1. Democrat 2. Republican 3. Independent, shifted around 4. Minor party or refused to say. Parents whould not say 5. Never noted, 'didn't get into parties,' Apolitical 6. Father didn't live in U.S. or wasn't a citizen, Didn't vote because he wasn't a citizen 7. Other 8. DK 9. NA

32 (IF VOTED) Have you always voted for the same party or have you voted for different parties for President? (IF SAME) Which party was that?

  0. (Always) same party—Democratic 1. (Always) same party—Republican 2. (Always) same party—other 3. (Always) same party—NA which party 4. Mostly same party—Democrat 5. Mostly same party—Republican 6. Mostly same party—other 7. Mostly same party—NA which party 8. Different parties 9. DK, NA, INAP

33 (IF PLANS TO VOTE) How do you think you will vote for President in this election?

  0. INAP., probably not vote, not vote, etc. 1. Will vote Democratic, for Humphrey 2. Will vote Democratic, for Humphrey, with qualifications 3. Undecided, depends, DK 4. Will vote Republican, for Nixon, with qualifications 5. Will vote Republican, for Nixon 6. Will (probably) vote for Wallace, American Independent Party 7. Will vote for other party or candidate. Progressive, Socialist, etc. 9. Refused to answer, NA 8. Refuses to vote for President

34 Now I'd like to ask you how you feel about some of the things people tell us when we interview them. Would you say that

most public officials care quite a lot about what people like you think, or that they don't care much at all?

    1. Care 5. Don't care 7. Refused 8. DK 9. NA

35   Would you say that voting is the only way that people like you can have any say about the way the government runs things, or that there are lots of ways that you can have a say?

    1. Lots of ways 5. Voting only way 6. No way to have a say 7. Refused 8. DK 9. NA

36   Would you say that politics and government are so complicated that people like you can't really understand what's going on, or that you can understand what's going on pretty well?

    1. Can understand 5. Can't understand 7. Refused 8. DK 9. NA

37   Are you married now and living with your wife (husband, or is he in the service)—or are you widowed, divorced, separated or single?

    1. Married and living with wife (husband—or husband in service) 2. Single 3. Divorced 4. Separated 5. Widowed 7. Common law marriage 9. NA

38   Are there any children under 18 years old in this family? (How many?)

    0. None under 18; INAP., coded 2 in Column 37 1. One 2. Two 3. Three 4. Four 5. Five 6. Six 7. Seven 8. Eight or more 9. NA

39   How many grades of school did you finish? Have you had any other schooling? (What was that?) (Any other?) (IF ATTENDED SOME COLLEGE) What college(s) did you attend? Where (is that/are they) located? Do you have a college degree? (IF YES) What degree(s) have you recieved?

    1. No more than 7 grades (possibly some non-college training) 2. 8 grades completed (possibly some non-college training) 3. No more than 11 grades but at least 9 4. No more than 11 (or less than 9) grades plus non-college training 5. 12 grades 6. 12 grades plus non-college training 7. Some college, AA 8. Bachelor's degree (4 or 5 years college) or higher 9. DK or NA

40-41   Respondent's main occupation—coded according to the

Duncan decile (Socio-Economic status of occupation).

00Lowest status

. . .

. . .

09Highest status

99DK, NA, score not available, housewife, student, member of Armed forces, disabled, etc. (The ranges can be set at 09 (Max.) and 00 (min.) if the researcher is not interested in the answer represented by 99.)

42   Do (did) you work for yourself?

0. INAP., R coded housewife or student 1. Yes, self-employed 2. No, not self-employed 3. Work both for self and someone else 8. DK 9. NA

43-44   Head's main occupation-coded according to the Duncan decile (Socio-economic status of occupation).

00Lowest status

. . .

. . .

09Highest status

99DK, NA, score not available (see 99 code of the question in column 40-41)

45   Head's main occupation—Do (did) you work for yourself?

0. INAP., Head coded housewife or student 1. Yes, self-employed 2. No, not self-employed 3. Work both for self and someone else 8. DK 9. NA

46   Does anyone in this household belong to a labor union? (IF YES) Who is it that belongs?

0. No, no one 1. Yes R (alone) belongs 2. Yes, head (not R) (alone) belongs 3. Both R and head belong 4. Someone else in household (alone) belongs 5. R and someone else in household belong 6. Head (not R) and someone else in household belong 7. R and head and someone else in household belong 8. DK 9. NA

47   R's social class—Which one class do you think of yourself as belonging to? Well, if you had to make a choice, would you call yourself middle class or working class? (IF MIDDLE CLASS) Would you say you are about average middle class, or that you are in the upper part of the middle class? (IF

WORKING CLASS) Would you say that you are about average working class, or that you are in the upper part of the working class?

0. Lower class 1. Average working class 2. Working class 3. Upper working class 4. Average middle class 5. Middle class 6. Upper middle class 7. Upper class 8. DK; uncertain of proper classification 9. NA

48   What social class would you say your family was when you were growing up?

1. Middle class 2. Working class 3. Upper class 4. Lower class, poor class 6. Refused to accept idea of classes 8. DK 9. NA

49-50   Are you a Protestant, Roman Catholic, or Jewish? (IF PROTESTANT) What church is that, Baptist, Methodist, or what?

00. Has no preference 10. Protestant general, e.g. Protestant, non-denominational 11. Protestant Reformation Era, e.g. Presbyterian, Church of England 12. Protestant Pietistic, e.g. Methodist, Church of the Brethren 13. Protestant Neo-fundamentalist, e.g. United Missionary or Protestant Missionary, Seventh Day Adventist 14. Southern Baptist, Missouri Synod Lutheran, other fundamentalist 15. Non-traditional Christian, e.g. Christian Scientist, Unity 20. Roman Catholic 30. Jewish 70. Greek Rite Catholic 71. Eastern orthodox 72. Non-Christians, other than Jewish, e.g. Mohammedan, atheist 79. Other religions 99. DK preference, NA

51   Would you say you go to church regularly, often, seldom or never?

1. Regularly 2. Often 4. Seldom 5. Never 9. NA

52   Here are four statements about the Bible, and I'd like you to tell me which is closest to your own view:

1. The Bible is God's Work and all it says is true. 2. The Bible was written by men inspired by God but it contains some human errors. 3. The Bible is a good book because it was written by wise men, but God had nothing to do with it. 4. The Bible was written by men who lived so long ago that it is worth very little today 7. Other 8 DK 9. NA

53   Have any members of your immediate family served in

armed forces in the past five or six years? (Who?) (Anyone else?)

1. (Yes), one or more sons or stepsons 2. (Yes), spouse 3. (Yes), father 4. (Yes), one or more brothers 5. (Yes), one or more grandsons or grandsons in law 6. (Yes), one or more sons in law 7. (Yes), one or more brothers in law 8. (Yes), nephew(s), grandnephew(s), cousin(s), uncle(s), other or NA who 9. DK, NA, No, none; no second or third response

Thermometer Questions

There are many groups in America that try to get the government or the American people to see things more their way. We would like to get your feelings towards some of these groups.

I have here a card (INTERVIEWER HANDS R CARD) on which there is something that looks like a thermometer. We call it a "feeling thermometer" because it measures your feelings towards groups.

Here's how it works. If you don't know too much about a group, or don't feel particularly warm or cold toward them, then you should place them in the middle, at the 50 degree mark.

If you have a warm feeling toward a group, or feel favorably toward it, you would give it a score somewhere between 50 and 100 degrees depending on how warm your feeling is toward the group.

On the other hand, if you don't feel very favorably toward some of these groups—if there are some you don't care for too much—then you would place them somewhere between 0 and 50 degrees.

The codes used in the "group thermometer questions" are the following:

00   Zero degrees, very cold or unfavorable feeling
15   Fifteen degrees, quite cold or unfavorable feeling

30	Thirty degrees, fairly cold or unfavorable feeling
40	Forty degrees, slightly cold or unfavorable feeling
50	Fifty degrees, no feeling at all about group; don't know much about them; DK, neutral
60	Sixty degrees, slightly warm or favorable feeling
70	Seventy degrees, fairly warm or favorable feeling
85	Eighty-five degrees, quite warm or favorable feeling
98	Ninety-eight, ninety-nine, or one hundred degrees, vary warm or favorable feeling
99	NA

Column
number

54-55	Big business—score on the thermometer
56-57	Liberals—score on the thermometer
58-59	College students—score on the thermometer
60-61	The military—score on the thermometer
62-63	Vietnam war protesters—score on the thermometer
64-65	Labor unions—score on the thermometer
66-67	Negroes—score on the thermometer

(For coding of columns 54-67, see codes used in the "group thermometer questions")

68-69   About what do you think your total income will be this year for yourself and your immediate family? Just give me the letter of the right income category (on this card).

10. Under $1000 11. $1000-$1999 12. $2000-2999 13. $3000-3999 14. $4000-4999 15. $5000-5999 20. $6000-6999 21. $7000-7999 22. $8000-8999 23. $9000-9999 30. $10,000-11,999 31. $12,000-14,999 32. $15,000-19,999 33. $20,000-24,999 35. $25,000 and over 97. Refused 98. DK 99. NA

70   Do you own your own home here, or rent, or what?

1. Own (or buying) 2. Rent (or lease) 3. Occupancy part of financial arrangement with employer or owner 4. Housing provided free by non-relative or NA if relative 5. Housing provided free by relative 6. Co-op apartment 7. Other 9. NA

71   Sex of R

1. Male 2. Female

72   Respondent's general interest in politics and public affairs seemed:

1. Very high 2. Fairly high 3. Average 4. Fairly low 5. Very low 9. NA

73   Respondent's general level of information about politics and public affairs seemed:

1. Very high 2. Fairly high 3. Average 4. Fairly low 5. Very low 9. NA

74   Are you people making as much money now as you were a year ago, or more, or less?

1. More now 3. About the same 5. Less now 8. DK 9. NA; no post-election interview

75   Who did you vote for in the election for President? (IF DIDN'T VOTE) Who would you have voted for for President if you had voted?

0. Voted, but not for President 1. Voted for Democratic candidate (Hubert Humphrey) 2. Voted for Republican candidate (Richard Nixon) 3. Voted for George Wallace 4. Voted for Dick Gregory, Pat Paulson, Eugene McCarthy, or write-in candidate 5. Voted for others 6. Non-voters 7. Non-voters, Humphrey, Nixon or Wallace preference 8. Non-voters, Humphrey and others, Nixon and others, Wallace and others 9. Voted, DK, NA for whom or refused to say

76   How about the elections for other state and local officers, did you vote a straight ticket, or did you vote for candidates from different parties? (IF STRAIGHT TICKET) Which party? (IF DIFFERENT PARTIES) How did you split it?

1. Voted straight ticket—Democratic 2. Voted straight ticket—Republican 3. Voted straight ticket—other party or NA which party 4. Voted split ticket—mostly Democratic 5. Voted split ticket—mostly Republican 6. Voted split ticket—mostly other party or NA how split 7. Voted split ticket—split evenly—Democratic and other, Republican and other, Democratic and Republican 8. Didn't vote for state or local offices; R says no state or local elections 9. Refused to say how voted, DK how voted, NA INAP., coded 6-8 or 9 in column 75; no post-election interview

77   Would you say that either one of the parties is more conservative or more liberal than the other? (IF YES) Which party is more conservative? Would you say the (R's/D's) are a lot more conservative than the (D's/R's) or only a little

more conservative? (IF NO) Do you think that people generally consider the Democrats or the Republicans more conservative, or wouldn't you want to guess about that?

1. Democrats a lot more conservative 2. Democrats a little more conservative 3. Democrats more conservative 4. Republicans more conservative 5. Republicans a little more conservative 6. Republicans a lot more conservative 7. Other 8. No, no guess, DK 9. NA

78   "Some people think it is all right for the public schools to start each day with a prayer. Others feel that religion does not belong in the public schools but should be taken care of by the family and the church." Have you been interested enough in this to favor one side over the other? (IF YES) Which do you think:

0. No interest 1. (Yes) schools should be allowed to start each day with a prayer 3. (Yes) pro-con, depends, both boxes checked, other 5. (Yes) religion does not belong in the schools 8. DK 9. NA, no post-election interview

79   In general, how satisfying do you find the way you're spending your life these days? Would you call it completely satisfying, or not very satisfying?

1. Completely satisfying 3. Pretty satisfying 5. Not very satisfying 8. DK 9. NA; no post-election interview

80   Generally speaking, would you say that most people can be trusted or that you can't be too careful in dealing with people?

1. Most people can be trusted 5. Can't be too careful 7. Other: depends; both boxes checked; refused to choose 8. DK 9. NA; no post-election interview